Theo-
logy
&
Life

THEOLOGY AND LIFE SERIES

Volume 2

Sacramental Realism

A General Theory of the Sacraments

by

Colman E. O'Neill, O.P.

Michael Glazier, Inc.
Wilmington, Delaware

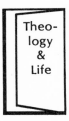

Theo-
logy
&
Life

ABOUT THE AUTHOR

Colman E. O'Neill, O.P., has been Professor of Systematic Theology since 1963 at the University of Fribourg, Switzerland. Previously he taught in Dublin and Rome. He has contributed to scholarly journals in Europe and America. Among his publications are *Meeting Christ in the Sacraments* and *New Approaches to the Eucharist.*

First published in 1983 by Michael Glazier Inc., 1723 Delaware Avenue, Wilmington Delaware 19806 • Distributed outside the U.S., Canada and Philippines by Dominican Publications, St. Saviour's, Dublin 1, Ireland • ©1983 by Colman E. O'Neill. All rights reserved. •Library of Congress Card Catalog Number: 82-084413 • International Standard Book Numbers: Theology and Life Series, 0-89453-295-2; Sacramental Realism, 0-89453-297-9 (Michael Glazier Inc.); 0-907271-21-9 (Dominican Publications) • Printed in the United States of America

CONTENTS

To
Maureen R. Healy

ABBREVIATIONS

Bettenson, *Early: The Early Christian Fathers*, edited and translated by Henry Bettenson; Oxford University Press, 1956 (fourth impression, 1978).

Bettenson, *Later: The Later Christian Fathers*, edited and translated by Henry Bettenson, Oxford University Press, 1970 (reprinted with corrections, 1977).

NR: *The Teaching of the Catholic Church as Contained in her Documents:* originally prepared by Josef Neuner, S.J. & Heinrich Roos, S.J.; edited by Karl Rahner, S.J. (= *Der Glaube der Kirche*, translated by Geoffrey Stevens), Alba House, N.Y., 1967.

Palmer: *Sacraments and Worship: Liturgy and Doctrinal Development of Baptism, Confirmation and the Eucharist,* edited with commentary by Paul F. Palmer, S.J., Longmans, Green and Co., London, etc., 1955 (Sources of Christian Theology, vol. I)

Biblical quotations are from *The Jerusalem Bible*, Darton, Longman & Todd, London; Doubleday, New York, 1966, (in which italics indicate quotations from, or close allusions to, another book of the Bible).

INTRODUCTION

IF IT IS TO BE ADEQUATE, a discussion of the Catholic sacraments aimed at developing a general theory has to draw on so many ideas from other parts of theology that it cannot avoid presenting itself as at least the outline of a complete theological system. This is because sacraments are particular events in the life of the church and the individual which bring into focus the entire mystery of salvation. Not only do they have ethical implications for those who take part in them; they also serve to give symbolic expression to the present activity of the creative and redemptive God who, in the Incarnation of the Word and the sending of the Spirit, reveals himself as a trinity of Persons whose purpose it is to share their own life with mankind. The sacraments stand at the point of intersection between the moral imperatives of the Christian life and the mystery of God who, in Christ, has taken the initiative in human history so that moral effort has to be seen as the human aspect of divine grace.

It is the community of the church that initiates sacramental action; and symbolic activity has a profound significance for the emergence of the individual as a person within the human community. For these reasons sacraments need to be considered as human phenomena, for it is through their anthropological structure that

9

they lead into the mystery of salvation. In the past twenty years or so it is this aspect of sacraments that has received the most attention from writers in Europe and the Americas. Not infrequently, however, authors who adopt such an approach seem quite unaware of the problems of theological method involved in submitting to an anthropological analysis an activity of the believing community. It can, of course, be done; but if it is to be done in a theological way, it is imperative to define precisely the relevance and the limits of the human sciences when they are used to clarify revelation. It is not enough to make a simple application of the current orthodoxy in sociology or psychology. That provides, if it is done properly, only the raw material for theology. The theologian has to interpret it and define its significance according to the principles of theology. This complicates things, for theological interpretation, no matter what intermediary techniques it may employ, always involves philosophical presuppositions; and the responsible interpreter needs to know what presuppositions he is working with and whether they are serious ones when it comes to doing theology. They may be such as to exclude from the start certain dimensions of the mystery held by the community's tradition to be essential. So far as I am aware, recent writers on the sacraments have not troubled themselves about this sort of self-examination; their interests have been more immediately pastoral or pedagogic. If this means, as I think it does, that a rupture has occurred between catechetical instruction and scientific theology, then this can only be to the detriment of both, but especially to the detriment of the former. Teachers and pastors should not be content to pass on the faith in terms borrowed from the human sciences for, if this is all they do, they are talking about man and not about what God does for man.

If this situation is to be remedied, pastoral theology of the sacraments needs to be rooted in serious systematic theology. It can neither make do with the expedient of group-dynamics technique nor adopt the self-defeating project of the German theological faculties of erecting itself into an autonomous "science," hardly distinguishable from the human sciences on which it draws.

This book is intended to be a contribution towards overcoming this undesirable situation. It is written from the point of view of systematic theology and attempts to provide a contemporary version of the treatise on the sacraments *in general*. In order to formulate general principles, it is necessary to examine in some detail the individual sacraments. Since it is general principles that are sought, the individual sacraments are not discussed in all their dimensions; for the same reason the complex history of the sacraments is referred to only where necessary and in a way that brings out its significance for the task in hand. What it is hoped will be found here is a systematic discussion of the Catholic theology of the sacraments, carried on in awareness of the ecumenical interest of this part of theology, but also concerned to discover in the tradition certain ways of thinking that the church of today and tomorrow should not be allowed to forget.

CHAPTER ONE:
SACRAMENTAL REALISM

IT IS NOT POSSIBLE to say at the outset of the enquiry all that is meant by "sacramental realism." It is only when the enquiry is completed that the sense of the phrase will emerge and that the claim implicit in it may be evaluated. The words, either separately or combined, can be used in several contexts, each of which would provide a different frame of meaning. Even if it is stated that "sacramental" refers here primarily to the sacraments acknowledged by the Roman Catholic Church, it still has to be explained what the term signifies for this community.

It is obviously easy to point to the list of sacraments and to the prescribed ritual forms and say that this is what we are talking about; but even then there might be some hesitation as to what exactly is being indicated by the term "sacrament of marriage," to cite a fairly evident example. It still remains necessary, in any case, to explain at some length why the community finds the sacraments important; and this is complicated by the fact that some of the sacraments are acknowledged by other Christian churches and their understanding of them does not always coincide in all particulars with what the Catholic tradition holds. Indeed, the ecumenical situation has modified, to a greater or less extent, the way in which individual Catholic theologians currently present their own tradition.

There is also a general tendency, confirmed by the Second Vatican Council, to move away from the special use of "sacramental," referring to certain rituals, and to apply the term to the church as a whole and to the person and action of Jesus Christ. This indicates how the notion of sacrament is used at a meeting-place of several theological topics and is intended to serve as a generalizing construct pointing to some characteristic common to many tenets of the Christian faith. In order to define the meaning of "sacramental" in its special use it is necessary to take account of the broader usage.

The second term, "realism," demands even more careful treatment. It is used by philosophers when they discuss theories of knowledge and then its precise sense inevitably depends on the system any particular philosopher is developing. In so far as it is possible to make a general statement about so indefinite a matter, it may be said that the term suggests that the system to which it applies claims to be able to account for real existence. This, however, can be done in all sorts of ways, most of them mutually exclusive, ranging from a logical deduction of reality from the idea (or Idea), as in classical idealism, to a simple affirmation of existence as unalterably resistant to any theory.

Theology and, indeed, faith itself are directly concerned by philosophical theories of knowledge since the truth-value attached to statements of faith is challenged by those theories and may emerge from the encounter either unscathed or radically modified. It matters very much to the believer, for example, whether the resurrection of Christ is interpreted by preachers and theologians as a subjective conviction of the disciples that Jesus' mission is of lasting significance, or as an objective event, even if it cannot be exhaustively described by analogy with ordinary historical events, or, finally, as something that calls for both of these approaches. A "realist" interpretation will certainly deny that any purely subjective understanding of the resurrection is adequate for Christian faith; but this still leaves room for a variety of explanations of its objectivity.

All this lack of precision flows into the combined form, "sacramental realism." So as to narrow the field let it be said that the intention here is to attribute to the system of special sacraments recognized by the Catholic church some measure of objective reality. Several accounts of this objectivity could conceivably be given. It is possible to stress the qualifying adjective, "sacramental," and explain the realism, wholly or in part, by the implications of communitary symbolic activity; this is an approach that enjoys considerable support among contemporary theologians who draw on the remarkable studies in this field being currently conducted in the human sciences. It is also possible, and it has been done in the past, to concentrate so much on objectivity, on, for example, the real presence of Christ in the Eucharist, that the qualifying term "sacramental" becomes redundant to the explanation.

There is at least one other possibility and it is one that appears more promising. While agreeing with the need to exploit fully the anthropological significance of the sacraments' symbolism, one can maintain that other categories, of a different order, are also necessary in order to describe adequately the kind of realism that faith ascribes to them. It is in the sense of this possibility that "sacramental realism" is being used throughout the present discussion. It might be objected already that, in comparing the first and third possibilities, a contrast has been implicitly set up between symbols and other categories or concepts, which is a false one. Symbols, it could be said, with their almost unlimited power of evocation, cannot usefully be opposed to concepts since these necessarily take the form of intellectual abstractions whose signification may quite easily be incorporated in concrete symbols. The cogency of the objection might easily be questioned by pointing out that theories about symbols, as distinct from symbols themselves, are also obliged to make use of abstract concepts and, as far as this goes, are on the same footing as any other theory; certainly, nothing guarantees that a set of concepts about symbols will be the right ones or adequate when the symbols are those of faith. However, it is more pertinent to state that the kind of realism or objectivity that is here being sought in the sacraments escapes the grasp of both concepts and symbols; for, even if it is impossible to talk about it without using concepts, as will appear, it is given and acknowledged in a judgment of faith which can be upheld only in the power of the Holy Spirit. In the case of the Eucharist, the clearest example, it will be maintained that two sets of statements are necessary to do justice to the mystery, the first set developing its symbolism, the second deriving from another, more radical, approach to reality.

This is not, however, a method that is relevant only to the Eucharist. It will be argued, rather, that the mystery of the Eucharist exercises a decisive influence on the whole project of the theological interpretation of the faith. This is because this one example of the kind of realism presupposed by the faith demands a general theory of faith-knowledge that is capable of accounting for it; and such a theory should be at work throughout the whole theological project. This does not, of course, mean that all the other truths of faith can be deduced from a general theory formulated in view of the Eucharist. What it means is that the kind of realism which is given in the Eucharist says something about the way God acts in the world and this establishes an openness on the part of the theologian to acknowledge other, similarly realistic, interventions of God. What they are can be known, evidently, only by revelation.

There is a further dimension to the phrase "sacramental realism" and it is one that needs to be stressed. It recalls the tradition originating in St. Augustine's development of St. Paul's teaching on baptism and the Eucharist. That tradition uses the categories, *sacramentum* and *res*, sacrament and reality, to express the relation that should exist between external things, words and actions, on the one hand, and true, personal participation in them on the other. Sacramental realism then denotes that kind of sharing in the words and ceremonies of the church which is authentic or "real." In order to develop systematically the pastoral significance of sacramental theology it is essential to begin, not with the objective realism of the sacraments, but with the realism of the Christian community's reception of Christ by faith. Once again, it is not possible to deduce the existence or the nature of the sacraments from a theoretical definition of the community. Their objective realism makes them something that, in one way or another, is given, to which the theory must be adapted and in which the life of the community is first fully realized.

The second sense of "realism" is equivalent to that of the more contemporary term, "personalism." The requirements of personalism, as it influences sacramental theology, are not confined to clearing up misunderstandings about what the Council of Trent was trying to say when it attributed to the sacraments efficacy *ex opere operato*. The efficacy attributed to the sacraments is subordinated to the efficacy attributed to Christ as Mediator of salvation. If sacramental personalism is to be understood, the question of the personalism of salvation must be resolved. Do not the traditional ways of understanding Christ's "merits" and "satisfaction" in our favor preclude true freedom or autonomy on our part? To answer this question negatively it is not enough to appeal to the inter-personal relations that should exist between the believer and Christ. That relationship is itself subsumed under the mission that Christ received from the Father and the mission of the Spirit, for without them it would not exist. Both sacraments and salvation through Christ stand under the mystery of the divine Trinity. Sacramental realism, if we are to perceive what it implies, requires that we make an effort to see it as an element in the mystery of God in his dealing with human personality.

Sacramental theology, it will be seen, can be properly presented only within a wider synthesis of doctrine. It is because contemporary theologians for the most part deny the feasibility of producing a synthesis in today's conditions that discussions about the sacraments are almost invariably divorced from wider theological considerations. Whether a synthesis is possible or not, any talk about the sacraments inevitably involves making a number of fundamental options about other theological matters. Some of these are made within sacramental theology itself; others are presupposed to it and need to be formulated first. The most important concern the doctrines of creation, providence and salvation; to these we turn our attention now.

CHAPTER TWO:
THE REALISM OF SALVATION

REALISM, when taken in the way St. Augustine suggests, as a correlative of sacramentalism is to be understood as having the same broad meaning as Christian personalism. If it sounds like an awkward substitution for a word that is already perfectly clear, the justification for its use lies in its implicit reference to the sacramental order. It indicates that Christian personalism, while it requires to be discussed in terms of human personhood, has traditionally had attached to it some kind of relation to sacraments, and that this relation too needs to be investigated. There is more to this than the simple requirement that ritual express the authentic Christian sentiments of those who take part in it.

If there is one thing that contemporary studies of symbolic activity have shown, it is that the human person comes to full development only by sharing in a whole network of social rituals which give the individual an identity within the group whose values he accepts as meaningful and contributing to self-fulfilment. This clearly points the way towards the possibility of integrating sacramental practice with authentic personal commitment. Equally, it imposes the obligation of thinking about sacraments in personal terms. When all has been said about the community that needs to be said, personalism still points to that inward freedom from external constraint or persuasion and from the individual's own self-destructive tendencies which is instinctively recognized as the mark of human maturity. Even if Christians believe that such freedom can be won only through living in the community called into being by Christ, it still remains a matter of individual decision and of an autonomy that can be sustained only by the individual.

Yet there are so many teachings of the Christian community that appear superficially to stand in the way of personal autonomy. It is not only the matter of laws and of Christian moral teaching. The conflict that these can occasion is resolved, in principle, by an appeal to the Spirit who writes the new law of Christ in the heart of those who receive him. The threat to autonomy seems to lie deeper than that in the Christian world-view. It is symbolized precisely in the sacramental system with its explicit claim to provide a space in which saving grace is given and its hardly concealed assumption that those who do not enter this space somehow constitute exceptions to the general economy of salvation. It is not hard to explain that the sacramental symbols of salvation are at the service of a deeper mystery and that the reality of salvation which they embody concerns all members of the human race since Christ's mission is to all. But that simply shifts the ground of the problem of human autonomy; for how can such universal significance be attributed to one man, unknown to so many, to so many more simply an example of one who discovered freedom for himself in the service of others?

Finally, when the Christian appeals, as he must, to the extraordinary belief that that one man has universal significance in an utterly fundamental way because he is the incarnate Word of God, then every human person, the Christian as well as the non-believer, is brought face to face with the mystery of God; and is not he the ultimate threat to the autonomy of others? All of these difficulties are finally resolved to this mystery, for the church, with her ministry of word and sacrament, claims to hold a commission from Christ to bring humanity to the Father through the power of the Spirit.

The sacraments should give meaning to life. It is right that they should be seen as celebrations of the human occasions of birth and marriage, of sickness and death, of service and, always, of communion; their symbolism provides a natural way of integrating the individual experience into the traditional wisdom of the community. But in and through all of this, the meaning that is being proposed is the one that God gives to his creation. Sacramentology must begin there, facing its ever-present assumption that God can give meaning to human life, that man does not deny himself by turning to God.

2.1 DIVINE PROVIDENCE AND HUMAN AUTONOMY

There is a romantic form of sacramentalism that sees God in the flower that springs up and blooms to perfection, untroubled by the perils of consciousness, or in the majesty of mountain ranges and the vastness of the sea, or in the innocence of childhood. Religious poetry knows how to weave such intimations of the infinite into awareness of the human condition with its hidden promises and secret terrors. Liturgies can be created that take up all that is beautiful in human experience and transform it into a new world that speaks of God and his coming to mankind. There is a sense, however vague, of divine providence in aesthetic appreciation of the world immediately around us or of the imaginative theories of astronomers and physicists.

Yet divine providence takes on existential significance only when it is related directly to human experience.

Something like that may be sensed in the colonies of seventeenth-century America, in the names the pioneers gave to their settlements, Salem and New Haven, New Ark and Providence itself. Perhaps it is found too in the project of founding commonwealths where political experiment was justified by the laws of providence; at least it proved when the experiment failed that human structures should not be too readily given divine authority. The intuition behind it was surely correct in its belief that providence, though it may sometimes be recognized in large events, is much more securely related to ethical behavior. To speak of providence in relation to the individuals who make up the human community is to speak of a personal God who is believed to be concerned about the individual's achievement as a person through the maturity that can be won only through moral decision.

In contemporary usage, providence brings to mind self-reliance and prudent care for the future. Careful investment is taken as a sign of responsibility and the very opposite of relying on others to take care of the future. When the religious person says that God is provident, he retains the image of looking towards the future in the sense that he attributes to God a concern for man's future. But he understands this to be a concern which is active now and which is making a positive contribution to the unique authentic possibility that man has of assuring his future, namely, his own personal development towards human maturity. He does not, therefore, understand his reliance on divine providence to be a diminution of his personal responsibility. The apparent paradox has always been resolved by the church in the simplest possible fashion—by living it.

When theologians made blundering efforts at producing a theoretical solution, suggesting either that God alone leads man to salvation or that, when all is said and done, man must make up his own mind, the church accused them of being rationalists, unperceptive of the mystery of God. His providential concern, though it is real, does not fall within human experience until it has been mediated by that same experience. If the theologian wants to talk about it, and he is obliged to do so, he must make it clear, first of all to himself, that he has to make use of two kinds of statement, both of which he takes to be true. He has to speak about man, his conscience and his full responsibility for his own moral choices. He has also to make statements about God; and this is much more difficult to do properly, not least because the only conceptual constructs the theologian disposes of to do this are drawn from human experience. It is necessary that he be acutely conscious of the transcendence of God if he is to recognize both the usefulness of human experience for opening the mind to the divine mystery and at the same time its radical limitations. Faith can do this sort of thing quite naturally as it does when faced with the deliberate simplicity of the parables of Jesus. Theologians, who are reflecting on faith, have to be much more self-conscious about it. So, for that matter, do those who find the paradox of a providential God who cares for fully responsible human persons to be meaningless. The kind of statement that is made about God is held to be compatible with the kind of statement made about human responsibility because the first refers to a reality which, by definition, does not suppress the reality of man. The mystery is, rather, that God gives being to man and to his freedom.

What is being said here is, clearly, a fundamental principle for the entire theological enterprise. It has to be invoked whether the subject is man or Christ or the sacraments. The kind of God being spoken about in Christian faith is one who, through Christ, creates freedom. Further, without in any way diminishing the role of Christ as unique mediator of salvation, the principle that God gives being to man must be read also in the inverse sense. Wherever authentic humanity, personal and communitary, is being painfully or joyously put together, it is a manifestation of God's providence. This is not the briefly popular "God of the future" whose personal identity evaporated in the practical details of social planning. It is the living God who may be called the "absolute future" of humanity only because he is active now in the fulness of his being.

What constitutes authentic humanity may not correspond in every way to what the self-professed humanist proclaims it to be, and the Christian church is obliged, in virtue of its mission, to make known its own values. These values, for the most part, are insisted on by Christians, not because of some peculiarity of their private dogma, but because they are held to be authentic human values, to be ignored at the peril of humanity itself. If there is a dogma behind this, it is one that is common to the Judeo-Christian heritage which maintains, with full awareness of the evidence to the contrary, that "God created man in the image of himself, in the image of God he created him, male and female he created them" (Gen 1:27). When the Christian church speaks of grace, the gift of God's love, it relates it to this primitive revelation and understands it to be a continuation of the primary gift of God which makes more profound the original likeness to the Creator.

This is an optimistic theology since it is turned to the initiative of God; the counter-balancing pessimism of the theology of sin, though it introduces a dialectic into Christian thinking, is not to be allowed to develop into despair or into the kind of Christian activism that refuses to recognize the hand of God wherever the human ideal is being realized. Authentic humanity, in spite of its fragmentary achievement at the individual and social level, is a manifestation of the living God.

This point of view needs to be developed, and not only as a basis for affirming that God's will of salvation is universal (cf. 1 Tim 2:4). It has consequences as well for those who have heard the gospel and belong to the Christian community. It is only within the context of the authentically human that the Christian can speak coherently of "grace," for grace is an abstract idea until it is incarnated in people who live by truly human values. The theological tradition of the Western Church, in its reflection on the mystery of grace, was often led into the discussion of subtleties whose meaning is intolerably difficult to grasp and whose relevance to Christian life is remote. In spite of this, whenever the tradition was directly in touch with the heart of the gospel, the main thrust of its teaching is directed towards showing how God's reaffirmation of mankind is realized from within the deepest resources of human personality.

The theology of grace does, indeed, accept as an axiom that God's purpose for man goes beyond the loftiest aspirations of autonomous humanism, for it accepts the literal meaning of St. John's promise: "We shall see him as he is" (1 Jn 3:2). In terms of this destiny the fundamental meaning of faith, hope and charity was worked out in terms of a God-centered personalism. Yet, just because it was God-centered, this personalism was perceived to be rooted in the creative depths of the individual and to be developed in community ruled by justice and love. Because God does not oppose man but give him his being, the grace that comes from God through the mediation of Christ respects the human situation so that it is both given, and assimilated by those who receive it, in a way that is utterly human. Since it penetrates to the depths of the individual its assimilation into the personality calls on all the resources of human decision-making and fidelity to self in spite of reverses.

Concern for God never suppresses truly human concern since God is served when man and his world are genuinely served. Moral decisions concerning the individual or the society he lives in lose thereby nothing of their complexity or their difficulty for, even when in prayer the assistance of God is recognized or sought, they must be truly personal. The Holy Spirit sent by Christ can make a saving entry into history only by way of such human, personal commitment which, though it is carried by the Spirit into the mystery of the Trinity, fulfils itself in the achievement of authentic humanity. The Spirit can do this and so be the Spirit who gives freedom (cf. 2 Cor 3:17) only because he comes as that creative power of God without which no commitment would be made.

If the Spirit is said to be given in other ways, for example in the sacraments, then these other ways must finally be brought into relation with that liberty which is his most radical gift. The theology of the sacraments, together with the ecclesiology and the christology it presupposes, can make sense only if they are developed in the light of a fundamental theology of providence and grace which recognizes the autonomy of man as a gift of the Spirit. The sacraments are celebrated only where there is explicit acknowledgement of the gospel; the mystery they are celebrating is being realized within the space they create for those who share in them; but it is being realized too wherever the image of God is emerging in the human race. To say that the sacraments must be celebrated when the gospel is acknowledged is not to contest the claim that the experience of grace arises most spontaneously where human beings meet each other as humans or when they are engaged in a personal search for self which reveals within them the traces of the image of God. Marriage, significantly, is numbered among the sacraments, at least in the Catholic tradition; this deserves thinking about for here Christian personalism is itself said to be sacramental.

2.2 MARRIAGE, SACRAMENT OF CREATION IN CHRIST

The fact that marriage gradually became accepted in the Christian tradition as a sacrament in the stricter sense is of special significance if we are trying to discover how personalism is related to sacramentalism. Leaving aside all the juridical and liturgical circumstances attached to the marriage ceremony, since they vary considerably throughout the history of Christian marriage, what is significant is that this most human way of living, entered into when the partners commit themselves to one another, is accepted in its complex existential reality as sacramental. There is no temptation in this case to place any artificial separation between the profoundly personal union of husband and wife and some kind of liturgical symbolism because it is the union itself that is sacramental. The fact that St. Paul was led from a homily on the responsibilities of married life to an apt citation from the *Genesis* account of creation—husband and wife are to be "one body" (Gen 2:24)—and from this to an allusion to the union between Christ and the church (Eph 5:21-33), is of less importance, suggestive though it is, than the affirmation of the church that marriage is in some outstanding way a possibility of grace.

There is something more to this than the simple observation that any state of life is to be considered as a vocation and a challenge to holiness, but it is not easy to say in a word what it is. It is clear that what is being spoken about is the married life itself with its human possibilities and dilemmas, its idealization in conflict with its realization, not only its joys but also its reverses, so long as they are subordinated to the overriding promises of fidelity. It is not difficult, seeing that the partners' personalities come to maturity in their mutual relationships, to grasp that husband and wife can be carriers of grace, one for the other; or that their situation of grace is broadened and made deeper through their children.

Certainly this is a very clear illustration of the way in which divine providence is at work whenever the promises that have been once made are not withdrawn. It is not only that this offers a lived experience of God's fidelity to mankind in spite of failure. It is the experience itself

and whatever joy or sorrow it may bring, whatever
decisions are made in favor of the other or in favor of both,
that present the utterly human face of the working of
providence. It is not unusual that the sense of being fully
human, fulfilled in a special way in parenthood, is
experienced as gift, as an excess of life which the individuals cannot account for as coming from themselves.
The Christian will call it grace and attribute it to God;
but the experience is not confined to the Christian. Here
the grace, if it is given, springs up from the life-giving
sources of humanity. It is recognized for what it is, a gift
of the Spirit of life, within the Christian community;
but awareness of it without the abilty to name its source
is more widespread.

When it is asked why the Catholic tradition should go
on from this and make it a formal point of teaching that
marriage is a sacrament in the stricter sense, then a question is being posed which is very relevant to the discovery
of what it is that fundamentally inspires the Catholic
tradition itself. The movements of Protestant reform
seem to have been based on an intuitive grasp of the
drama of sinful humanity which, if grace is not brought
to it through a new initiative of God, is doomed to self-
destruction. The great Scholastics of the Middle Ages
were equally convinced of God's absolute initiative in
Christ even though they lacked the literary verve of the
Reformers and their existential awareness of the dialectics
of human life. But for some of the Scholastics, at least,
the mystery of Christ did not constitute the fundamental
intuition of their theological method. They were much
closer to the historical roots of Christianity in the Jewish
tradition where the God of the Alliance is such a God
because he is the creator God; he is a God who can shape
history and intervene in it because he is the God who
called the universe out of nothing.

The doctrine of creation, in its theological form, is a
subtle one; but its influence on Catholic teaching is

far-reaching and easy enough to recognize. It enabled
the great thinkers of the Jewish and the Christian tradition, over the centuries, to transform the Supreme Good
of Plato and the Unmoved Mover of Aristotle into the
living God of Moses and of Jesus. This was not because
they felt themselves authorized to dispense with revelation
in their theological systems; that would have been a
psychological impossibility for them. Rather they
recognized in what was for them the summit attained by
pagan thinking a human heritage which, if it was modified by the doctrine of creation, would permit them, in
their turn, to think about the God of Christian revelation,
just as it had aided the theologians of Islam. The subtleties evidently make themselves apparent in this grafting
of the achievements of human thought onto the root of
revelation.

St. Thomas Aquinas, taking up a position that was
bitterly contested in his time as an illegitimate importa-
tion of Aristotle's paganism, could declare that what the
Christian means by creation would remain a viable
concept even if the world had no beginning (*Summa
theol.*, I, q. 46). He accepted as a matter of revelation that
the world did, in fact, have a beginning because the
Creator willed it to be so; but he insisted that, no matter
what hypothesis might be made about the origins of the
universe in the physical sciences, the doctrine of creation
would stand because it is concerned with the necessary
dependence on God of the kind of existence enjoyed by
the universe. Since it is the limitations of experienced
existence that cry out for God, his creative activity is
needed, not just, as the imagination might fancy, at the
beginning, but at every moment that such existence
continues. It may be noticed in passing that existence,
in the strong sense here intended, is not, and can not be,
taken into account by theories of evolution which, by
definition, are based on physical observation.

It is the affirmation that the Father of Jesus Christ is the Creator, and the constant reference to this basic principle, that are distinctive characteristics of Catholic theology. It is true that the principle is not always to the fore in contemporary theology since a great deal of effort is being devoted to the deployment in theology of the contributions of the human sciences; and, as far as this goes, there is not very much appreciable difference between theologians of different Christian communities. It still remains that if a theology is to be representative of the Catholic tradition it will be one that is looking for a synthesis of thinking about revelation and thinking about the affirmation that God is the Creator.

The Catholic tradition thinks the way it does about marriage and affirms it to be a sacrament, not because of a positive act of "institution" attributed to Jesus, but because it understands salvation in terms of creation. It regards marriage as the most fundamental form of human association and, in that sense, as an "institution" given by God the Creator. It sees it, consequently, as blemished by sin, just as all human relations are; and it sees Christ's redemptive work as a force acting towards the restoration of marriage to its pristine ideal. To call this a sacrament is equivalent to a whole theology about the relation of Christ to creation, of grace to the human task.

The sacrament is not a blessing conferred by a representative of the community on an otherwise purely human occasion and human undertaking. The blessing is from Christ himself and it comes from within the human reality; the mission of the Word incarnate is to renew the man and woman, the image of God, created through the divine Word. Why marriage should be singled out in this way and said to be a sacrament when other forms of life in Christ are not, can be due only to the fact that married life corresponds most closely to the design of creation. Celibacy can be justified only by appeal to the values of the new Kingdom. On the contrary, the coming into being of human persons, both the partners and their children, in an ambiance of human communication lies at the very well-spring of that self-communication of God by which he gives life through creation and through grace. When Christ speaks of marriage it is to recall what it was "from the beginning" (Matt 19:8), what it could be discovered to be if the implications of marital promises were worked out according to their intrinsic significance. His words were addressed to people who had allowed that vision to fade because their way of life had blinded them to the uncompromising character of that giving of self that is implicit in the consent of marriage.

To speak of a specifically Christian sacrament of marriage is to speak of how Christ, when he sends the Spirit, makes it possible for man and woman to find within themselves the original dynamism of life as the basic gift of creation, to allow it to realize its power for human maturity, and to know that by giving themselves to this mystery they are growing into the Kingdom of God. God's creation is good; his forgiveness restores its joy; marriage is a sacrament because it, in its unique way, makes this known. In this way it is a source of grace, first for those who share in it, then for others.

In marriage, realism or personalism merges with the sacrament so that the two are not distinct. It is for this reason that the example of marriage serves so well to illustrate the principle that the two should never be separated. It is, of course, necessary, to see more closely what is involved in the sacramentalism of the other sacraments but the need to correlate it with personal involvement remains constant. The sacrament of reconciliation or penance is closest in this respect to marriage since in it too what is important grows out of the heart. Here it is sorrow for sin which, while it can only be a gift of divine grace, is at the same time one of the deepest decisions we can make and one that, if it is to be effective, must engage our whole lives.

Yet even here, in penance, where personal involvement is so profound, there is an element apparently extrinsic to our commitment in the ceremony of absolution; and the same thing is to be observed in the other sacraments. It is, doubtless, correct to say that what is being cele-brated in the other sacraments is the salvation brought by Christ to his community, the church, and this calls for symbolic action expressive of the community's dependence on Christ. This places the sacraments in their ecclesiological and christological context. We have already noted, however, that this does not resolve the problem of personalism; it simply raises it again, this time in terms of the salvation brought by Christ.

Neo-scholastic theology, which flowered briefly in the Catholic church at the turn of the present century, thought it could solve the problem by referring to the "merits" and "satisfaction" of Christ in favor of the church. The words were taken from medieval theology but, divorced from their background, they served as little better than tokens for thought. It is, indeed, possible to give an account of the Christian faith by saying that Christ merited grace for all mankind and satisfied for all sin; this is a workable solution until the problem of Christian personalism makes itself felt and the question is asked as to how it can be reconciled with a doctrine of mediation expressed in juridical terms. Providence, it has been said already, manifests itself in fully human decision-making. How can this be reconciled with a christology of the sacraments which speaks of the applica-tion to the individual of the "objective redemption" won for all by Christ? Here is another presupposition of sacra-mentology that needs to be thought about.

2.3 PERSONALISM AND REDEMPTION

2.3.1 *The theory of "merit" and "satisfaction"*

The Christian who makes use, to describe what he owes to Christ, of symbols such as "meritorious passion and death" or "satisfactory sacrifice" knows quite well that the mystery he accepts in faith is not such as to reduce his own life to being a shadowy reproduction of something that has really and truly occurred only in the history of Jesus Christ. He is well aware that his faith begins to take on sense only when his own free will acknowledges his obligation to follow the teaching and example of Christ; and he knows that this involves all the uncertainty that any human life contains.

He learns that, though he attributes to the suffering of Christ a unique significance, his own suffering and that of the world go on. He will have to come to terms with the final paradox that, though he holds that Christ won victory over death, he himself and those he holds dear are not exempt from death. His faith makes it possible for him to accept his created existence and to take it in hand in as fully responsible a way as he is capable of. It still remains that his faith goes out to the individual person of Christ and not to a vague life-force manifesting itself in the struggle to be human. His faith leads him to recognize that the project of being human is not within his own grasp; this is the experience of what St. Paul, particularly in the *Letter to the Romans*, calls sin and understands as the reason why both Jews and gentiles must look beyond themselves to the God who offers them gratuitous justification. Recognition of this incapacity to be human is a first opening of the human heart to the need for a new divine initiative, one that can only take the form of an act of divine love, trumphing over sin and restoring creation to its God-given purpose.

Because it is God's, this new initiative of love is creative just as is the love that calls man out of nothingness. It may be called an act of mercy or forgiveness of sin; but these concepts need to be freed of the juridical overtones which they still retain even when we apply them to God. As a symbol that evokes recognition of God's love, forgiveness is properly applied as a name for his initiative;

still, it should not be taken to mean that the Father chooses to ignore sin. Divine forgiveness, since it is an act of providence, is active; it creates in man the means by which he may bring order out of disorder; it creates love where there was hatred.

Faith in Christ as mediator between sinful man and the Father needs to be thought through in the light of the creativity of the Father's forgiving love. The New Testament itself betrays how difficult it is to escape from more or less juridical ways of thinking about this mystery which involves the depths of persons, both human and divine; and juridical analogies for it recur throughout the Western tradition.

The term "mediator" has itself a juridical origin. The New Testament corrects the kind of legal reductionism that this could give rise to by its simple appeal to the mystery of love which permeates all that Christ does; but this leaves the task of systematic theology unfinished, for the way in which this love led to Christ's suffering and death still needs to be accounted for. An existential reading of St. John, for example, which brings out the gospel's stress on the inter-personal relation established by faith between Christ and the believer, can be only part of the truth. It correctly underlines the demand made by Jesus for personal dedication to his ideals and to his person and the believer's response is rightly seen as a gift of the Spirit.

But an existential analysis, because it employs only the categories of individual encounter, stops short of an account of Jesus' mediatorial suffering and death. St. Paul's interpretation of mediation goes further when it postulates so intimate a union between Christ and believers that together they form one body, that is to say, one person; but even then Christ is spoken of as the head of the body in order to preserve his unique mediation of salvation. The question still remains as to how Christ can be accepted as mediator without the believer renouncing his own responsibility for his sin and for his own necessary growth in personal maturity.

When the pre-Reformation theologians spoke of Christ's merit and satisfaction they were, indeed, offering a solution to the question just posed but they were doing so in a context where, in their account of the life, passion and death of Jesus, they were taking very seriously the dogma of his true humanity. Because they were doing that, they were able to use categories they had already developed in their theology of the Christian life. They had consequently already recognized that the terms, "merit" and "satisfaction," are juridical in character and, if to be used analogically of the Christian life, need to be modified very radically in their significance. The major adjustment that had to be made derived from the truth of faith that attributes to God all saving action, while maintaining man's full responsibility as man. Merit was transformed from an impossible mercantile claim to recompense against God into personal growth in likeness to God, the divine initiative in this being presupposed. Christian satisfaction was removed from the context of penal justice and became, at least as far as the present life is concerned, that personal form of self-discipline which, when inspired by love, aims at eradicating whatever it is that impedes that God-given growth.

It was also necessary to transcend a narrow concentration on the perfection of the individual that might be suggested by this form of Christian personalism. In fact, although the possibility of doing this was already suggested by the appeal to the role of love in satisfaction, the truly communitary dimension of the image of God and its growth could be systematically developed only after the terms "merit" and "satisfaction" had been used to describe the human activity of Jesus. When they had been extended to that unique case, they acquired a fulness

of meaning which was seen to be revelatory of the communitary nature of all Christian life. Needless to say,
it is not immediately apparent what the terms signify
when they are extended to the saving activity of Jesus and
a special difficulty attaches to the idea of satisfaction,
not least because misunderstandings about it make it, for
practical purposes, unusable today.

In spite of this, it is worth while to try to go beyond
the strangeness of the terminology of an Aquinas and
ask whether the approach he suggests to the mediation
of Christ might not be helpful when the question is raised
whether or not acceptance of that mediation, through
faith and the sacraments, involves renunciation of
responsibility on the part of the believer.

Two main lines of thought need to be pursued, corresponding to two aspects of Christ's mediation and the way
in which it benefits the believer. The first is concerned
with his mediation of divine life or growth into the image
of God. The second, closely allied with the first and
possibly, from the point of view of experience, the more
easily understood, has to do with the actual conditions
in which the Holy Spirit is sent into a world marked by
sin or by forgetfulness of God.

2.3.2 The Mediator of divine life

To say that Jesus Christ is mediator of the divine life—
this is the first line of thought—is to say something about
the personal life of this man and the effect it still has
on others. He is held to have realized, in his life and in
the way he met his death, all that is meant when it is said
that man is made to the image of God. His was a life
filled with the Spirit and centered on his Father and for
this reason turned towards the Father's design of loving
concern for man and all creation. His love for his Father
and his service to his design gave his life that harmony
with all that is good that was expressed in his every contact

with those he naturally called his brothers and sisters
and finally in his sufferings and death. The fact that he
encountered almost universal opposition to all that he
lived for has no need of explanation. This is the way in
which mankind reacted and still reacts to his intolerable
message with its promise of true human freedom as a
gift from God.

What distinguishes the person of Christ, in Christian
belief, from all those other figures of history who have
embodied the authentically human as flowing from
union with the Creator is that Christ is held to be a
unique person, one whose human achievements can affect
other men in a way which no other historical figure can
possibly achieve. It is not simply that his love is "con-
tagious," as existential theologians like to put it. It is
certainly this, but that is the property of true love and,
in its own way, of true conviction wherever they are to be
found. On the contrary, when Jesus said that he was to
offer himself "for you," for all mankind, he is understood
in the Christian tradition to be saying that his love for
the Father and for mankind shares, in a mysterious
fashion, in the creative power of God's own love. It is a
love which serves the divine love in such a way that it can
bring into being love in other men. In a way, perhaps,
even this could, at the limit, be applied to all human
love for all love can evoke, though not always, a responsive
love in another. The Christian tradition means to affirm
this about Christ's love since his love works in human
ways; but it means to affirm much more than this because
it believes that Christ truly sends the creative Holy Spirit.

This extraordinary claim implies that the creative
providence of God, which enables men to be free and so to
love, acts through the love of Christ in a way that cannot
be explained in terms of human love. It is a claim made
about no other man that he, as the Greek Fathers put it,
"divinizes" his followers, restoring them to their true

humanity as images of God, called to see God. The Christian community could find no other way to account for this unheard-of belief except by saying that Christ is the incarnate Word of God who has authority from the Father to send the Spirit. This was no abstract theorizing about the pre-existence of Christ; it was the only way to account for the Christian experience of Christ's power. The theories came only afterwards.

If we follow this line of thinking about how Christ's human love shares in the creative power of divine love we begin to grasp the force of the assertion that Christ and those who believe in him form, in a certain sense, one person. There is, of course, implicit in this expression the affirmation, made throughout Scripture, that salvation comes about only within the community of believers. But something more than that is being said about the personal unity of the Christian community, for this depends on the unique person of Christ. The phrase, "one person," aims at overcoming whatever traces of juridical thinking may still cling to other traditional phrases about Christ. Phrases which refer to Christ's taking our place or making satisfaction for our sins betray the fact that they focus on the sufferings of Christ; even if they do not, evidently, eliminate consideration of the love which inspired his suffering, they do shift the emphasis away from it.

In order to cut through any strand of thinking that appeals to Christ's substituting for others, it is important to isolate the central theme of his mediating love; and this is what is done when the phrase "one person" is introduced. Attention is then directed to the unity of all Christians and, indeed, of all men, which is brought about by the fact that their love of God and of each other is given to them by Christ. The question of suffering, whether Christ's or that of others, should be approached only when that central truth has been assimilated.

The divine love, always a creative love in the strict sense of the term, is the source of Christ's universal love and then of all authentic human love. The tradition expresses this when it names Christ the mediator of the New Alliance. Yet there is something left unsaid in this title, something which the notion of "one person" tries to bring out since it contains a reference to the freedom and responsibility of those who benefit from Christ's mediation and from the creative love of God.

When Christ enters as our mediator he does so within the context of that divine providence which, while being the creative source of all that is truly human, does not suppress individual freedom but rather makes it possible. If one were to concentrate exclusively on the individual's responsibility, the mediation of Christ would be obscured. If, on the contrary, one were to concentrate exclusively on the mediation of Christ, the individual's freedom might seem to be compromised.

The theological effort, necessary to preserve the two poles of the situation is summarized in the phrase "one person." Because all are inspired by the same Spirit there is a harmony of will that is characteristic of the unity of a person. Because it is Christ who mediates the Spirit in virtue of his mission from the Father the unity of all flows from his unique person and this unity goes beyond that of the psychological order. It is christological, referring back beyond the humanity of Christ to the person of the divine Word who encompasses all that is created. It is, for this reason, ontological, belonging to the order of being that is the gift of the Father of creation. An existential reading of the gospels, which underlines the human encounter between Christ and the believer, has its own usefulness; but the freedom of the Spirit, given by Christ, must be grasped at a more fundamental level as God-given power that permits man to achieve his God-given destiny.

There is something emerging from this enquiry that has far-reaching consequences for our understanding of the mystery of Christ. We began with a line of thought concerning Christ's mediating role in the gift to believers of the divine life, something suggested by the medieval concept of "merit." This is now seen to refer to an activity of Christ that is rooted in the mystery of the creative and redeeming Trinity. It is now possible to discern the fact that there is something not quite right about the way the question is being put when it is asked how Christ saved us and how it is that his salvation does not diminish our personal responsibility. Going a little further, there is something not quite right about according a certain autonomy to a section of theology and labelling it "Christology," as though Christ could be considered without constant reference to those who believe in him.

Theology should never, in fact, isolate Christ from believers; nor should it isolate believers from Christ. That neo-scholasticism, to look no further than recent Catholic thought, could construct, within the context of its Christology, a theory relating to "objective redemption" is an example of the kind of artificial isolation we are thinking of. "Objective redemption" was intended to signify the work done by Christ on earth in so far as it won salvation for all; it was then asked how this is conveyed to individuals. There is every reason to think that over-emphasis on St. Paul's "once for all" in relation to Christ's mediation is another such example.

There is no question, evidently, of denying the need to consider what is unique in the existence and the activity of Christ. The correction that needs to be made concerns precisely the theological habit of introducing an artificial separation between that unique activity and its active mediatorial function. In positive terms: the full significance of the unique work of Christ can be appreciated only when it is seen in conjunction with the actual influence it brings to bear on those who believe. It is almost a truism to insist on the believer's dependence on Christ; time should be taken to think out what this means in terms of Christ's relation to believers.

Failure to maintain in theology the real bond which permanently relates Christ to believers leads to the use in his respect of patently juridical notions such as that of the "treasury" of his merits and satisfaction; these are, at best, temporary pegs for thought and they need to be instantly adjusted. To speak, as even the medieval Scholastics did, of Christ's having "merited" salvation for us is to pause for breath when half-way up the hill. A preliminary statement has been made and it is not inaccurate; but by itself it is incomplete and, probably, a source of misunderstanding. It is necessary to maintain the thought that has been set in motion and to anchor it firmly in the reality of what Christ does for believers.

His real activity as mediator is not achieved, even as mediation, until it actually bears fruit in the free behavior of those who believe in him. It will not, therefore, be fully achieved until history has run its course. Talk of Christ's "merit" for his members remains a half-thought or a juridical abstraction until we refer his action to some actual example of the reception of his work by a believer. To divorce the two moments, to be content with the verbal distinction between objective and subjective salvation, is to run the risk of making out of Christ some kind of magical being who has already lived out the reality of the individual Christian's personal history. When believers receive from the creative love of God the liberty of the Spirit and take up, in full human responsibility, the conduct of their lives, then this is through the mediation of Christ. His life and teaching, his suffering and death, all that makes him human, this was what was needed to bring into the world the true image of God and to bring it, in the person of Christ, in a creative way that would spread out from him, in the power of the

Spirit, to affect all those who believe or even seek to believe. It is by a theological artifice that one aspect of this mystery is singled out and called merit.

2.3.3 The suffering of the Mediator

A second line of thought has already been suggested, complementary to the one just followed; it has to do with the actual conditions in which Christ mediates the Holy Spirit and so takes into account humanity's sinful state. Nowhere does the temptation to isolate Christ from the rest of men appear more clearly than in the theological discussion of Christ's suffering and death, conceived as redemption. There is an endless series of theories about this, most of them subtle variations on the theme of vicarious satisfaction. St. Anselm of Canterbury, who in the eleventh century, by a stroke of genius, set the terms for the discussion ever since, clearly centered his thought on the scriptural witness that Christ suffered "for us." He went on from this to an analysis of the personal value of the actions of the God-man; here he introduced a juridical analogy which, whether it is accepted or rejected, has succeeded in anchoring much of subsequent theology to a theoretical distinction between the event of Christ's passion, now terminated, and the results of this event in the community of believers.

His suffering is interpreted as being of such great personal value that it outweighs the offense offered to God by the sin of all mankind. The redemption thus achieved is then to be communicated to individuals through faith and baptism. There are obvious difficulties about this account of redemption when the personal responsibility of the believer becomes a central issue. Once again they have their origin in the separation that is taken for granted between Christ and those who believe in him. Once again there appears to be a possibility of overcoming the difficulties if the separation is not maintained.

St. Paul, who in his letters is much taken up with suffering, both his own and that of the churches he is addressing, does not acknowledge the separation of that suffering from Christ's. It was he who went beyond the kind of narrative theology contained in the synoptic gospels' account of the passion of Jesus and who developed a more systematic view of the significance of the scandal of the cross. He was guided by an intuitive grasp of the consequences of the union that exists between Christ and his members. He saw this union primarily as giving significance to all the events of Christians' lives; but he also saw it as the key to the mystery of Christ's death on the cross.

Paul habitually appeals to this union when he wants to make the point that divine love has established a pattern of suffering, death and resurrection in the existence of Christ which is to be reproduced in all Christians according to all the variations of their individual histories. *Romans*, ch. 8, contains one of the most striking passages in this sense; but this type of faith-assertion is a standard argument for St. Paul. Less frequently and perhaps less clearly, the argument from unity in Christ operates in the inverse sense; then the sufferings of Christians, which are of immediate experience, become a way of understanding why Christ should suffer. The importance of this, if a personalist interpretation is to be given to the "satisfaction" of Christ, requires some explanation.

One of the most illuminating suggestions is made by St. Paul when, speaking of his trials as a missionary apostle, he says: "It makes me happy to suffer for you, as I am suffering now, and in my own body to do what I can to make up all that has still to be undergone by Christ for the sake of his body, the Church" or in literal translation, "to make up all that is lacking from the sufferings of Christ" (Col 1:24). It is clearly St. Paul's view that the Christian missionary, because he carries on the work of Christ, must also share his sufferings, and that even this

works in favor of his converts. This does not, however,
exhaust the implications of the daring suggestion that
something is, in fact, lacking from the sufferings of
Christ. Such a suggestion can legitimately be made only
if there is a strong sense of the unity that exists between
Christ and his members. The sufferings of the members
are not simply a sharing in the same fate as that of Christ;
they make a positive contribution to his sufferings.

St. Paul is at times quite willing to make a rapid
allusion to the sufferings of Christ which is strongly
juridical in tone as when he says: "For our sake God made
the sinless one into sin, so that in him we might become
the goodness of God" (2 Cor 5:21). The second part of
the phrase fits into a context where he is speaking of the
apostolate as being "all God's work" (v. 18). Since this
forms the main line of his thought, the first part of the
phrase, interpreting the cross as a vicarious penalty for
sin, needs to be read in the light of that. The part that
suffering plays in the mystery of divine love cannot be
sought first in the person of Christ himself for he was
sinless; nor will it do to say that the Father transferred
to him the punishment due to mankind's sin.

Indeed, if we are to grasp the meaning of suffering as
somehow incorporated into a design of divine love, we
have to go beyond the purely penal evaluation of it that is
usually assumed in the Anselmian tradition. A positive
significance can be attributed to suffering, that of Christ
and that of those who believe in him, only if it is related
to the condition of the human race, placed as it is in an
environment whose physical laws can lead to individual
and social disaster and in a society where sin has corrupted personal relations and where the individual is
himself corrupted.

Christianity is not to be made an ideological justification for human suffering but it does maintain that all
evils, other than sin, can be made an occasion for good—
and even sin can be called in the liturgy a "happy fault."
In *Romans*, ch. 8, St. Paul appeals to "the glory which

is waiting for us," which outweighs present sufferings; but this eschatological hope for respite is seen as an integral part of the process by which believers in Christ become, in accordance with the Father's love, "true images of his Son" (vv. 18-30). Now, men become images of the Son not by suffering but by the Spirit; and yet suffering can play its own role in that development. This is, first of all, because suffering, on any realistic view, plays a part in Christian as well as in any other life. More importantly, it is because the image of the Son is being reproduced in those who belong to a society marked by sin and who are themselves involved in the difficult task of overcoming sin in their own persons.

Though St. Paul laid so much emphasis on the adoptive sonship given through faith and baptism, he was only too well aware that this, besides being a divine gift, imposes a whole series of obligations which indicate the way in which true freedom lies. The baptized Christian and the Christian who shares in the Eucharist are not persons who, in all honesty, can see themselves as a totally "new creation." It is within this dialectical situation, where the new and the old enter into conflict, where the image of God is restored yet the one who bears it is paradoxically still attracted by sin or suffers from its indulgence, that suffering can be freed from the negative, juridical implications of the term "satisfaction" and be given personal value in Christian growth.

The tradition of asceticism, when it has not been divorced from the good news of the gospel message, has always recognized this. Yet this intuition into the demands of Christian life has not been consistently developed in terms of its consequences for understanding the sufferings of Christ himself. This is, perhaps, not surprising, for suffering cannot play the same role in the life of Jesus as it does in the lives of Christians. For the Christian, growing into the love of God can hardly be other than painful while the personal disorders resulting from sin are being set right; but Christ was without sin, the perfect image of the Father. It still remains that the unity which exists between Christ and believers suggests that the only way in which Christ's sufferings can be properly interpreted is if they are given ethical significance by the sufferings of others, of sinners who have received the Spirit through the mediation of Christ.

The only ethical meaning that can be attached to the term "satisfaction," in the sense of making recompense for an offense against God, is the reference to personal development just outlined. It follows that Christ had no need of such satisfaction. It is useless to revert to the mythical notion that his sufferings could have had some kind of value in the sight of his Father which could be set against the punishment due to sinners. It is also inadequate to appeal to the Old Testament theme of the Suffering Servant, poignant though this may be, for it too relies on the imagery of heroic self-sacrifice for the sake of the people. It is, perhaps, unwise of Christian theologians to rely too heavily on this theme in their christologies, without making it clear that the Old Testament can supply only analogies which need to be radically modified when they are applied to the mystery of Christ.

To say that Christ's love explains everything can only lead to the question why the Father could not have chosen some other means than the passion to bring his creative love into the world; and questions of this kind, which abstract from revelation, can lead only into a theological blind-alley. Where all these explanations fail is in their unconscious assumption that it is legitimate to consider Christ's own person without, at the same time, associating him with his members. This is contrary to the principle already enunciated that Christ and his members should never be isolated from one another. His mystery is revealed only in them and comes to its fulness only in them.

It is time now to bring together the two lines of thought we have been following, the first concerned with Christ's bringing into the world the divine creative love, the second seeking to account for the suffering associated with that mediation because the world is sinful. It was possible to maintain the strictly personal character of faith in Christ's mediation by referring to the divine initiative in his person, for it is this divine initiative that is at the root of true human freedom. Within the relationship thus set up by the Holy Spirit suffering takes on its only possible ethical significance.

On the side of the believer it becomes a means of personal growth into likeness with Christ by love. The suffering itself, whether chosen as a means of discipline or accepted when it comes unbidden, is satisfactory, not because it propitiates an angry God, for this is incompatible with the Christian conception of God, but because it has an essential role to play in the achievement of Christian maturity. On the side of Christ there is only the excess of love which led him to share in the destiny of mankind. For him suffering was not a way to maturity but a manifestation of the fulness of the image of God.

Within the divine Trinity there can be no trace of suffering, only a fulness of creative love that, having given mankind its being, knows what must be done if a sinful world is to be restored to communion with the divine Persons and within itself. The divine Word, containing within himself the Father's design for creation, restores creation from within his own humanity. In this incarnation it is possible for the Word to suffer with all those who share in humanity. His was a freely accepted suffering whose true significance is realized only when to it is united the suffering of those whom the Spirit joins to Christ. It is the whole suffering of the world which is lacking from the sufferings of Christ; but the sufferings make up what is lacking only when those who bear them are able, through the love which comes from Christ, to make use of them for the purposes of that love.

It is in this existential union with Christ that those who believe in him allow his sufferings to become actually

redemptive. Once again, the distinction between "objective" and "subjective" redemption is seen to be inadequate to the reality of the "one person" who is Christ
with his members. Christ's "for you," though it represents the utmost gift of his earthly life, has not achieved
its immanent purpose until it becomes "in us" when the
suffering he accepted out of pure love becomes a suffering
that we accept because it can help us to overcome whatever it is that still obscures the image of God in humanity.

Within the one person of Christ and believers, marked
as it is by the totality of Christ's unselfish love, the sufferings of believers too may take on a significance that is
not restricted to the individual. There is a mysterious
commerce among the members, sustained by the Spirit. It
is never possible that any individual be exempted from the
demands of personal growth of Christian maturity, but
the community of believers can contribute, in numberless ways, to the creation of conditions which make that
growth a less daunting project. St. Paul could point in
his own apostolate to one of the more dramatic ways in
which this comes about. The love of Christ, shared with
his members, has its own way of knowing which ways
will serve.

This whole discussion of Christ's mediation was made
necessary because a theology of the sacraments cannot
simply take for granted "conclusions" held to be authorized by the arguments proper to christology. If the sacraments are said to apply to individuals the "objective
redemption" won for all by Christ, as it is commonly put,
then failure to examine the meaning of redemption can
only import into sacramentology a theological shorthand
which gives an illusory solution to problems created by
the community's belief in the efficacy of the sacraments.

Chief among such problems is the apparent paradox
contained in the two complementary assertions that
divine providence never suppresses human responsibility,

and that the sacraments make available to the individual the mediation of Christ. In order to resolve the paradox it is necessary to show that neither Christ's "merit" nor his "satisfaction" for human sin—to use the accepted terminology—excludes the whole normal process of personal growth in acceptance of Christian values. To retain the terms "merit" and "satisfaction" and to explain them in reference only to the past acts of Jesus, as though his mediation of salvation were an accomplished deed with present, barely conceivable consequences for believers, is to give an account of the mystery of salvation that is radically incomplete. Christ may never, in fact, be separated from those who, by believing in him and receiving his Spirit, discover their own human autonomy in its authentic challenge. Whenever he is separated from believers, the terms "merit" and "satisfaction" begin to echo with the resonances of their juridical origin and Christian personalism becomes, theoretically at least, an impossibility.

It is only too easy to parody the incoherence of a theology that allows itself to slip into this position and contemporary theologians are quite frequently ready to amuse their readers by doing so. A more responsible way of dealing with a long tradition is to translate the seemingly juridical terminology into a language that speaks of the initiative being taken by the Father in Christ for our present salvation.

The divine creative love enters the world through the humanity of Christ, through his life, passion, death and risen person, and is in this way active now in the world to restore the image of God in humanity. Where this love is active suffering can provide a new dimension to the mystery for it can make us like Christ, not by simply sharing in his fate as though suffering were no more than an accident of personal history, but by our personal acceptance of an experience which is needed to overcome the restraints within ourselves that hold back the development in us of the image of God.

This is a sharing in the sufferings of Christ that gives *them* their full significance, for without the sufferings of those who believe, accepted for what they can achieve in terms of personal maturity, the sufferings of Christ can be explained away as nothing more than the consequences of his contemporaries' rejection of his message. In this way Christians fill up what is wanting from the sufferings of Christ, namely, their own often painful growth in his likeness. It is for this reason that, when the symbolism of the sacraments opens out the community to receive Christ as mediator of its salvation, it is, by that very fact, inviting those who share in it to make his mediation a reality in their own lives.

CHAPTER THREE:
THE SACRAMENTALISM
OF SALVATION

CHRISTIAN PERSONALISM has been analyzed in the preceding chapter in terms of its ultimate mystery where human freedom is seen as a gift that only God can give. Such freedom, given by the Spirit, is not to be confused with arbitrary choice nor with makeshift accommodations of moral purpose to passing circumstances. It can only be understood if human destiny and happiness are acknowledged by faith to lie in God himself and if freedom is consequently seen to be authentic only when a person's decisions are in harmony with an inner dynamism towards God that lies hidden in God's creature. Analysis of this kind is indispensable for reflection on the implications of Christian liberty; but Christian existence itself, because it is a lived experience, is rarely reflective in this way. It follows its own kind of rules that are seized more readily in terms of psychological and social factors, though it remains Christian only when the reference to true happiness in Christ is maintained.

It is through human contacts that a person comes to know himself and change himself; in this way too he hears the word of God and slowly learns what that name means to him. The sacraments of the church, especially the Eucharist because of its frequent celebration, provide a way of experiencing and re-examining and experiencing again what it is that God is saying to his people. At the heart of all this, even though it may not always be clearly felt since the Christian, just as much as others, is involved in a web of sometimes conflicting motivations, there has to be a fundamental openness to God and to his working. This is a deep-rooted listening to God or for God that can gradually, and working according to its own rhythm, bring influence to bear on a whole life-style in a world that imposes its own secular concerns. There may well be personal inconsistencies within this fabric of Christian life or, at times, outright incoherence because every new situation makes conflicting claims even on the committed Christian. The mystery of providence and freedom is woven into the pattern of daily life, not always recognized or even recognizable, yet, once discerned or discerned anew, giving intimations of meaning to human existence.

Christ himself finds his own place in this complex pattern. In his words and actions, as recounted in the gospels, he speaks of his Father, whether in simple parables or dramatic paradoxes, and brings to the misery of the human condition the healing that only the Spirit can give. In this way, which led to his passion but also to his resurrection, he is believed to have brought into history nothing less than the decisive act by which God restores fallen humanity to its true destiny.

Contemporary theologians, when they want to sum up the whole meaning of the event of Jesus Christ, have taken to using a cryptic phrase which is intended to express both the historical mission of Jesus from the Father, culminating in his resurrection-ascension, and the sending of the Spirit to the assembly of believers.

They speak of Christ as the "archetypal sacrament"—though English-speaking theologians sometimes prefer the more mysterious *Ursakrament,* possibly because it is difficult to translate. The adjective "archetypal" is chosen here because it indicates that the term has a background of idealist thought with its echoes of Platonism.

3.1 CHRIST AS ARCHETYPAL SACRAMENT

The point being made in this description is that God's graciousness to man takes on definitive shape in the human existence of Christ and that it becomes effective when Christ is received by faith as the one who is sent by the Father to bring the Spirit. This is sacramentalism in its most basic form for it is here equivalent to Incarnation, even if the sacramental approach, precisely because of its neo-platonic overtones, lacks the dogmatic precision of St. John's "the Word was made flesh." When the person of Christ is placed in this way at the source of the entire sacramental order, and when the church, in its turn, is viewed as a general sacrament, subordinate to Christ, of the divine saving mercy, the individual sacraments are freed from their isolation as unconnected rituals. They are taken up as integral parts of an economy of grace in which God becomes immanent in his creation so as to bring it to himself.

The Latin word "sacramentum" was first used by Tertullian (c. 200 A.D.) as an appropriate way of expressing the "oath" taken by the baptized when they swore allegiance to Christ, and the Latin tradition has always found it difficult to escape from the legalistic resonances of that word. The more theological connotations brought to the word when it is applied to the whole economy of salvation are important in themselves and have the advantage of more closely approaching the depth of significance attached to the notion of the mysteries in the Eastern churches.

It may well be a question whether this is the most apt theme to choose as the dominant one in an account of what Christianity means today when Platonic ways of thinking are not notably widespread in the industrialized West. It is understandable that it should appeal to theologians consciously influenced by German classical idealism for it offers a general conceptualization of the Christian mystery which permits the "logical deduction" of the church from Christ and of the sacraments from the church. This kind of systematic thinking appears to be more useful as a possible framework for a final synthesis of salvation theology than as its starting-point. If the complex notion of sacrament, archetypal or subordinate, is to have existential content, it has to be built up from personal experience of the church's ministry of word and sacraments and from the more concrete ideas that this varied experience gives rise to. This seems to be corroborated by the parallel situation which occurs when Western thinkers are faced with the Eastern theology of the mysteries. This theology presupposes a lived experience of the Orthodox liturgy which, however much it may be honored by them, is very largely inaccessible to those whose perceptions are formed by the liturgy and theology of the West.

What is meant by saying that Christ is the archetypal sacrament may perhaps best be approached by way of the theology of St. John. Apart from the "signs," that is, the miracles presented by John as significant for an understanding of the ministry of Jesus, there is a whole series of accounts which speak of the reactions of individuals who came into contact with Jesus; simply what these people say shows the human side of the sacrament. St. John orchestrates his whole gospel with these personal reactions, some negative, some positive, some simply bewildered, some pregnant with mystery, some bad-tempered; but all are provoked by the behavior of Jesus who, for his part, moves serenely through the crowds, confident that he speaks for the Father and acts in his name. A seemingly trivial remark of his moves Nathaniel to intone: "Rabbi, you are the Son of God, you are the king of Israel" (1:45-51). A more human situation is summed up by the earthy woman of Samaria and then by her townspeople: "Come and see a man that has told me everything I ever did; I wonder if he is the Christ . . . . We have heard him ourselves and we know that he really is the saviour of the world" (4:5-43). A court official grasps at a straw: "Sir, come down before my child dies" (4:46-54). A man cured after lifelong illness knows only that he has found someone with authority to abrogate the sacred law of the sabbath: "The man who cured me told me, 'Pick up your mat and walk.'" "The man had no idea who it was" (5:11, 13).

After the loaves have been multiplied, the people are caught up in the Mosaic symbolism of the event and salute Jesus as "the prophet who is to come into the world" (6:1-15). When he speaks clearly of his mission from the Father and promises that it will be fulfilled in the Eucharist, most of the people do not understand but Peter speaks for the Twelve: "Lord, who shall we turn to? You have the message of eternal life, and we believe; we know that you are the Holy One of God" (6:22-66). Freed from the rigors of the Law when her accusers are obliged to admit their own guilt, the woman taken in adultery acknowledges her liberator: "No one, sir" (8:11). Accused himself of being possessed by a devil, Jesus protests at the blasphemy: "I do nothing of myself; what the Father has taught me is what I preach; he who sent me is with me, and has not left me to myself, for I always do what pleases him . . . . Before Abraham was, I am"; for this, they take up stones against him (8:12-59). A man born blind, aggressively protective of himself even after he has been cured, finally bears witness before the opponents of Jesus: "Ever since the world began it is unheard of for anyone to open the eyes of a man born blind; if this man were not from God, he could not do a thing"; and, almost against his will, he is forced to ask Jesus: "Tell me who he is (the Son of man) so that I may believe in him." "You are looking at him; he is speaking to you"; and the man said: "Lord, I believe" and worshipped him (9:1-38). Among the people the debate continues. Some said: "He is possessed; he is raving"; others: "Could a devil open the eyes of the blind" (10:20-21). At the raising of Lazarus from the dead, the already dramatic scene is raised to universal significance when Jesus says: "I am the resurrection." The sacrament is complete when Martha responds: "I believe that you are the Christ" (11:25-27).

In scenes such as these, Jesus manifests the coming into the world of the power of the Father; and those who meet him react in all the variety of ways that are open to their human individuality. They are episodes that spell out in existential detail the theme announced by John at the beginning of his gospel: "The Word was made flesh, he lived among us, and we saw his glory, the glory that is his as the only Son of the Father, full of grace and truth" (1:14). Their deepest meaning is expressed in the discourse of the Last Supper when the mission of Jesus is set against the eternal dialogue between Father and Son in the Spirit that is the creative source of salvation (13 - 17). A moment of transition occurs when the risen Christ entrusts his disciples with the earthly representation of his continuing mission of grace, and for this gives them the Spirit whom they are to bring to others. "'As the Father sent me, so am I sending you.' After saying this he breathed on them and said: 'Receive the Holy Spirit. For those whose sins you forgive, they are forgiven; for those whose sins you retain, they are retained.'" (20:22-23).

It is all of this that is meant when Christ is said to be the "archetypal sacrament" of salvation, as he makes known the Father by revealing his own relation to him and by giving effect to his mercy for mankind. To the Father he says: "Glorify your Son so that your Son may glorify you; and through the power over all mankind that you have given him, let him give eternal life to all those you have entrusted to him . . . . I have glorified you on earth and finished the work you gave me to do" (17:1, 4). St. John, who was so possessed by this intuition into the meaning of Christ's mission, never tires of bringing into sharp focus the mystery of the Word's taking on human features. "Something that existed from the beginning, that we have heard, and we have seen with our own eyes; that we have watched and touched with our hands: the Word, who is life—that is our subject. The life that was made visible: we saw it and we are giving our testimony, telling you of the eternal life which was with the Father and has been made visible to us" (1 Jn 1:1-2).

Though the light shone so brightly for John himself, his gospel admits that Jesus and his message were ambiguous, that they made no sense to those who did not wish to hear of a Father such as Jesus tried to reveal nor to respond to him as Jesus did. The sacramentality of Christ can be discovered only by those who accept him for what he claims to be; and it is only in this reception and in all that follows from it that the sacrament is complete; for what the incarnate Word made manifest about his relationship to the Father was that it is fulfilled only when those who believe in him share in it. Here, once more, we encounter the mystery of grace where all depends on the individual's response to Christ and all depends on the gift of God: "It is my Father's will that whoever sees the Son and believes in him shall have eternal lie, and that I shall raise him up on the last day. No one can come to me unless he is drawn by the Father who sent me, and I will raise him up on the last day" (6:40, 44).

When the sacramentality of Christ is said to be archetypal, the implication is that the pattern of his earthly existence is to be reproduced in all those who are drawn to him by the Father. This reference to earthly existence represents a clear break with the kind of symbolic thinking associated with the Platonic tradition. The latter's archetypes function within a system which, in a desperate attempt to resolve the problem of evil, locates outside the material world of sin and falsehood the "really real," the true, the beautiful and the good. These become ideal archetypes, held to embody all those qualities sought after by the heart of man but which are not to be found, or only fleetingly, in the world of immediate experience. Salvation from evil, can only be found, if at all, by purification from the bonds of materiality and by desire for union with the ideal. This represents one of the classic solutions to the human dilemma, and yet it bears witness only to the capacity of the human spirit to extend itself and to construct within itself an idea of the infinite. It can do so only at the expense of denying its own roots in the material world and in human history; and, after all that, it has no guarantee that its ideals are any more than the counter-image of its own despair. The central doctrine of Christianity explicitly rejects this dualistic view of the world with its powerful but ineffective symbolism, for the Word was made flesh and it is in his human existence that salvation is to be found. The fleshly realism of Christ, the incarnate Word, is made effective by the initiative of the Father who fulfils the ineffective longing of the human heart and himself draws the sinner to Christ. The pattern of Christ, this unique archetypal sacrament, is reproduced when the Christian cleaves to the human situation and transforms it by the power of the Spirit.

3.2 THE MYSTERY OF CHRIST

In the theology of St. Paul there appears an emphasis on a new dimension of sacramentality, for the starting-point of his reflections is to be found in his own experience of the risen Christ and of the communities which grew out of his own preaching in association with the church of Jerusalem. The details of Jesus' earthly life are not referred to; instead, the broad events of his death and resurrection, seen as the source of Christian life and worship, occupy a central position.

The first chapter of the *Letter to the Ephesians* offers a striking summary, in the form of a song of praise, of this Pauline theology and it is here that the Christian economy is seen as the Mystery of God's saving will now revealed and active. The passage shows the link uniting christology with ecclesiology since the reflections it contains are set in motion by a consideration of the meaning of the Christian community in which the people are brought together by faith and baptism. A list is given of the blessings conferred on the community of Christians in accordance with the eternal plan of the Father. Nevertheless, the logical development of the thought goes from the Spirit conferred in baptism, mentioned at the end of the list, to the death and resurrection of Christ which make that gift possible, and then to the Father's merciful design which is the source of all. St. Paul can speak so confidently of the hidden purpose of the Father, the Mystery, because it has been finally revealed in the raising of Christ from the dead which, from the author's point of view, marks the turning-point in history when the Spirit was released to carry out his work of transforming the whole of creation. He can affirm that this purpose is now affecting the lives of Christians and will continue to do so until they are united with the risen Christ because of the very fact that they have received the Spirit through faith and baptism.

The divine plan that is revealed can be accounted for only in terms of the absolutely gratuitous love of God, for he has determined that "we should become his adopted sons, through Jesus Christ for his own kind purposes, to make us praise the glory of his grace, his free gift to us in the Beloved" (1:5-6). For St. Paul this goes beyond anything that had been openly promised to the people of God whose alliance came through Moses, and therefore beyond any promise that was implicit in creation. An interjection is made at this point, adverting to the non-freedom of sin which forbids our allowing God's purpose to be realized in us; but this is dismissed almost as an interruption to the flow of thought: in Christ, "through his blood, we gain our freedom, the forgiveness of our sins" (v.7).

The dominant theme is the "richness of the grace," that is, the gratuitousness, of the love of God for us (v.8). What adoptive sonship means and what therefore is the content of the Mystery is stated in terms inspired by the cosmic significance of the resurrection of Christ. For St. Paul, this was no isolated event concerning only Christ himself as an individual. It was so much bound up with a new insight into the designs of God that St. Paul had to recast all his thinking about the revelation made to the Jews. He now could grasp the awe-inspiring fact that the age-long alliance between God and the Jewish people had, all at once, passed out of the bounds of the book of the Law, passed beyond even the law of love that it contained, and had taken living shape in the person of the risen Christ who sends the Spirit and so makes love possible.

He now could see too that this concentration of saving power in one person, the Son, meant that the Father, who had raised Christ from the dead, would finally act in like fashion with those who belong to Christ and, indeed with all his creation, making it, as Christ's person is now, the bearer of his Spirit. "He has let us know the mystery of his purpose, the hidden plan he so kindly made in Christ from the beginning to act upon when the times had run their course to the end: that he would bring everything together under Christ, as head, everything in the heavens and everything on earth" (vv. 9-10). If Christ has thus become the final and personal expression of the alliance, it follows that the Jewish people implicitly "put their hopes in him before he came" (v.12) and that now Christians have entered the alliance of love because they have been brought to Christ by faith. This they did when they believed the good news preached to them and "were stamped with the seal of the Holy Spirit of the Promise, the pledge of our inheritance" (vv. 13-14), a reference to baptism.

The notions of archetypal sacrament and of Mystery are complementary. Each is so full of significance that the terms pass beyond the precision of conceptual constructs that might be attached to them and become symbols, evocative not only of vast stretches of thought but also of the response that those who believe should make to them. The first has its origin in an immediate experience of the living Jesus who passes into the state where he gives the Spirit after his ascension to the Father, an experience passed on to others by the Twelve. The second derives from the experience of adoptive sonship given through the Spirit in the community of the baptized. From this it points to the inward being of God himself, to the Father who is made known through Christ and who gives himself through the Spirit; and to his eternal design of love to associate all creatures with himself by their union with Christ.

Christ is the archetypal sacrament because, in his human existence, with all that it implies, he stands always in relation to the Father and to the Spirit and so brings the divine mystery into history. As personal sacrament, he is the mystery incarnate in its fulness and therefore as the source of its extension to all who believe in him. By speaking of him as sacrament, we find the way already opened to introducing that new form of sacramentality that is given in the church.

This new sacramentality has, first of all, a reference to the Blessed Trinity, for it is the continuing historical shape that is given to the mystery of Father, Son and Spirit as it unfolds in succeeding generations. In addition, it bears a particular reference to the incarnate Son, to the one person, known in his earthly existence as Jesus, who now lives in glory; for it is he who is the unique Mediator, communicating to those who believe the life of the Blessed Trinity.

3.3 THE CHURCH AS SACRAMENT

It has not been possible to speak of Christ without speaking at the same time of those who receive him as the one sent by the Father to restore creation to its original purpose and to allow men to share in his own sonship by the power of the Spirit. Christ as Mediator must be seized in all his living act of self-communication as he brings the present community of believers into active being through the Spirit he sends. In its turn, even more evidently, the gathering of those who believe in the Mystery can never be understood for what it is, if it is separated from the Mediator and his mission from the Father. The cornerstone of the whole structure of the church is, therefore, the belief that the crucified Christ rose from the dead and is now living with the Father, for it is the reality of his risen person, who with the Father sends the Spirit, that makes this belief, not a blind acceptance of something that lies hidden from us, but truly the beginning of eternal life within us.

The restoration of creation, of the human race and the material world, which for us remains a promise, at present only partially fulfilled, is affirmed to be already fully achieved in so far as it concerns the person of Christ. It is because he is in this state of achievement that he can send the Spirit on those who believe so as to fulfil his mediatorial role by making them adoptive sons, destined to share in his resurrection. The Catholic belief in the assumption of Mary, while it makes a statement about her personal resurrection, serves too as a symbolic affirmation that concerns the whole church, called like her to share in her savior's victory over death.

The New Testament uses many symbols, taken for the most part from the Old Testament, to express the living union that binds together the crucified and risen Christ and the church. They are symbols that reflect an agricultural economy with its simple arts and, as well, a religious spirit formed within the Jewish heritage of an alliance with the Lord which has affinities with marriage and which points, however obscurely, towards a universal brotherhood of men (see Vatican II, *Constitution on the Church*, nn. 6 & 7). What lies behind the symbols is the conviction that the man of Nazareth, because he is truly living, not just in memory but in the fullest sense of the word, is here and now present and active within his community, binding it to himself.

It matters very much as far as the credibility of the community is concerned and even more as far as its own being is concerned, if the community does not always or in all its members give adequate testimony in its way of living to this extraordinary claim; but this does not change the fundamental conviction that gives the church its meaning. In its preaching and worship the early church was conscious of the fact that its whole reason for being lay in its union with the living and life-giving Christ, for only in this union could it approach the Father. It was only natural that the community was consumed with a desire for the fulfilment of that union, but also that it should proclaim it to the world.

The picture becomes much more complex and, in places, obscure as the church grows older and its members find that they are just as much involved in the ambiguities of history as anyone else, even though they know that it is the vocation of the Christian to resolve those ambiguities in the light of Christ. Those who govern the community are most easily faulted, within the church and in public opinion, if their service to the ministry of Christ leads them into a labyrinth of political skills where they become imprisoned in their own techniques. But all the members are equally exposed to the temptation of establishing a compromise between what they profess and what they decide is liveable in their own circumstances. It still remains that the principal theme of their belief is clear: that their authentic life as Christians, to the degree that they accept the responsibility of following the preaching and example of Jesus, flows directly from the present influence exercised on them by the risen Christ and the Spirit who gives them their freedom. This is the Mystery in its present form, turning on the humanity of Christ, with the community, while it lives by the Spirit, looking back to Christ's earthly mysteries and looking forward in hope and love to the future mystery of the Kingdom of God in its fulness. It is this that is at the heart of whatever symbolic language may be used by the church when it speaks of itself in the Scriptures, in its worship or in its formal creeds.

The church is reminded that the risen Christ is central to its existence whenever it celebrates the Eucharist. Emphasis needs to be laid on this fundamental Christian experience of the sacrament, for in it is given the person who links the present community of believers with the early community that set down an account of its origins in the Scriptures. This establishes between people of very different cultural backgrounds a common understanding that is prior to techniques of literary interpretation. It is the awareness of the presence of the risen Christ that draws together into unity the diverse threads of the faith professed in the creeds. It is this experience that the church has of its union through the Eucharist with the risen Christ that guides the church in its self-understanding. In this way the symbols used in the Scriptures of the church are to be interpreted in the light of the church at worship in union with Christ.

To talk about a symbol, if the talk is logical, is to make the symbol disappear together with its evocative power. This can be avoided if one symbol is clarified by appealing to other symbols, which is what is done in biblical theology and, very largely, in preaching. As soon as the attempt is made to go on from this to any sort of systematic statement of the faith, the theologian is obliged to translate the symbols into logical structures making a claim to express truth. In this he risks what seems success at the expense of filtering out much that contributes to the original vitality of the symbols. Further, because the symbols enshrine the many-faceted experience of being Christian, it is not unusual for a theologian to single out for clarification only some of the possible significations of a given symbol. Those who live by the gospel will instinctively recognize that something important has been left out, even if they feel that they are not qualified to refute the theologian's reasoning. This instinct of the faithful is not something that can be formulated from the results of an opinion poll; it is bound up with experience of the risen Christ in the Eucharist.

The symbol of the church that has been most expressive of its self-understanding since the Second Vatican Council is that of the "people of God." The symbolism is weighted towards the pilgrim status of the church. It turns the attention of theologians to the anthropological significance of the faith, and the service of Christians towards the Christ who continues to suffer in his brothers. This turning towards man, whether in reflection or in action, is profoundly Christian, for the people of God is nothing if not human and humanitarian. It is, however, only when there is exlicit advertence to the fact that this people is formed in the Eucharist and through the Spirit of the risen Christ that a theology of man and a mission of justice and peace become authentically Christian.

The reference to Christ returns explicitly, though in a phrase that owes more to theological reflection than to symbolism, when the church, in a way that recalls what is said of Christ himself, is said to be sacrament. The Council's *Constitution on the Church* (nn. 2-4), uses a mosaic of scriptural texts to spell out in terms of each of the Persons of the Blessed Trinity the divine action which brings the church into being. It concludes with the words of St. Cyprian who, in the third century, said of the church that it is "a people brought into unity from the unity of the Father, the Son and the Holy Spirit," thereby developing the cryptic phrase already used (n. 1), terming the church "a sacrament, that is, a sign and instrument, of communion with God and of unity among all men." The word "sacrament" is here given a reference to the life of the people of God that recalls the sacramentality of marriage; it is the total life of the community, to the degree that it is inspired by Christ, that is the Mystery of salvation in the world. The Christian life, contemplative and active, in its secular occupations as well as in its worship, is itself the realization of the Mystery and the human means by which the Mystery extends its reach; for here the mediation of Christ is recognized, accepted and celebrated and is transposed into the commitment of Christians.

The Eucharist is an integral part of this living sacrament and, indeed, without it, there would be no church to serve as a sign of salvation. Yet, though the Eucharist unites the community with the risen Christ, and brings into focus all its varied activities, the church is not properly understood as the sacrament of Christ alone. It would be misleading to interpret the analogy between Christ as sacrament and the church as sacrament as though the latter were, as was sometimes said, a continuation of the Incarnation. The papal title of "vicar of Christ," commonly used since the time of Innocent III in the thirteenth century, was misleading in this sense and is now little used. Christ is unique as mediator and as archetypal sacrament. If he personally enters the church in the Eucharist and in other ways, this is because he continues to exercise in person his role as mediator. In this role he is turned towards the mystery of the Trinity and towards those he brings into that mystery. The church, therefore, is the sacrament of the

Blessed Trinity itself. In order to be that, it professes its faith in Christ who alone has the power to send the Spirit in virtue of his mission from the Father. Here are two dimensions of the sacramentality of the church that need to be explored. The first is given because the divine Trinity is drawing the members of the human race into communion with its own life. The second refers the church in a special way to the incarnate Word since it is to him that the church looks as the way into the heart of the Trinity. This second dimension links the church with the historical Jesus and with this same person in his present glorified state.

3.3.1 Sacrament of the Trinity

The earthly mission of the Word and the visible descent of the Spirit on the church at Pentecost both point towards the ineffable mystery that lies at the origin and at the end of the whole economy of salvation. At beginning and end is the divine Trinity's giving of itself to its human creature through such an excess of life that this human person, made in the image of God, can be brought to see God as he is, to know him in the Word and love him in the Spirit. This ultimate mystery that enfolds Christ and the church can too easily be passed over as not relevant to the ethical demands of Christianity, though, in truth, without it, the ethics would be without lasting meaning.

It is not impossible that, by dint of constant repetition, the term "faith in Christ" might be trivialized. Even when we try to give words like "salvation" or "liberation" all the breadth and depth that the gospels give them, we find it hard, at least in the modern Western world, to hold our attention on the center of the mystery which was expressed by St. Athanasius, bishop of Alexandria during the fourth-century debate about Christ, as follows: "The Word was made man in order that we might be divine" (*On the Incarnation*, 54; Bettenson, *Early*, 293). This is what faith in Christ finally requires that we accept, not because its daring proposal puts our credulity to the test, but because the word of Christ itself, received in faith and expanding into love for what that word contains, is already the germ within us of the life of the Trinity made over to us.

The Spirit who is sent does not simply bear witness to the saving efficacy of a salvation wrought long ago in Christ. He is a sanctifying Spirit who gives us the freedom to believe and to love and so to make salvation our own lived reality. At his coming the three divine Persons live in us, not in a spatial sense, though it is legitimate to imagine it in that way, but through our own living movement of faith and our love for the Father and all that he has created. In that knowledge and love, springing as they do from the depths of our own being, there grows up the created image of the Blessed Trinity. This is more than a mark left by the creative Trinity on its handiwork; it is the very life of the Christian and is meant to grow towards maturity even though it is subject to all the fluctuations of the human situation.

"If anyone loves me," says Jesus, "he will keep my word, and my Father will love him, and we shall come to him and make our home with him"—this in reply to the understandable question: "Lord, what is this all about? Do you intend to show yourself to us and not to the world?" (Jn 14:22-23). He answers in his own way, pointing to the mystery. He will show himself, and therefore the Father from whom he comes, to the apostles and to all who believe, because his word, implanted in their hearts by the Spirit and "kept," grows into what can only be described as a communion of life with the life of God himself.

To accept Christ for what he is, in terms of his message of hope, is to accept the Father who sends him and to know that their meaning is love. St. Augustine, struggling with the impossible task of describing the inward life of God, points to this image of God inscribed in the person of the believer. His thought alternates between the image and the exemplar, drawing from each, as the thought progresses, fresh light to illumine the other. "The word we are seeking to evoke" he puts it at one point, "is knowledge accompanied by love" (*On the Trinity*, Bk. X, ch. 10; further texts in Bettenson, *Later*, 234-6). For once Aquinas, commenting on this, surpasses the concise eloquence of his mentor: "As for the Son, he is a Word, yet not an ordinary word, but the one who breathes love—*Verbum, non qualecumque, sed spirans amorem*" (*Summa theol.*, I, q. 43, a.5 ad 2).

What is being spoken about is the Trinity itself, in which knowledge and love are at that intensity of perfection where the union with the other that all love seeks is given in an identity which does not suppress the difference of persons. The *way* in which this unfathomable mystery is being spoken about is structured according to what does lie within the experience of the saints, namely, their own being as image of God in which the three divine Persons make themselves known. They make themselves known, not in themselves, but through the word of Christ received in faith and nurtured so that it becomes authentically a part of the believer's own being, reflecting all that he is, issuing one might say, from the depths of his own being as it comes from the Father of creation. Such a word about God cannot be purely theoretical; it is of its nature to be caught up in a movement of love which has its origin in God himself but is shared in by the believer who receives the Spirit. In the eternal self-communication through knowledge and love that constitutes the hidden richness of the life of the one God, is to be discovered the pattern and the meaning of creation and salvation. If man is called to reproduce the pattern in his own person and in his community, he can do so only if that divine Trinity draws him into its own life, making his knowledge and love of God a created image of itself.

All the individualism that is inescapably bound up with the Christian calling is reflected in the doctrine of the divine indwelling. Nevertheless, this growth of the person in the likeness of God is made possible only within the community formed by the incarnate Word. The secret withdrawal to the depths of the mystery that the indwelling implies is centered on a contemplation of a word that must break out into a love like that of Christ, one that reaches out to all that God has made in the Word.

The church is the sacrament of the Trinity because it is the assembly of those who confess the mystery and who are called to live it and to let it live in them; because the word that it preaches is the word of the saving Trinity; and because its worship and sacraments are offered in praise of the Trinity which gives itself to the church. As sacrament of the Mystery, the church is not separated from the rest of mankind for the sacrament is the place where the mystery of all men is explicitly recognized and explicitly made a measure of true humanity. The mystery itself is at work wherever that true humanity is being realized, wherever the Spirit is secretly active even though the word of Christ is unacknowledged. The integral sacrament of the Trinity, however, is to be found only where the full heritage of Christ, the unique Mediator, is received and proclaimed in the assembly. Here, the sacrament of the Trinity bears a special relation to Christ and his mediation.

3.3.2 Sacrament of the Mediation of Christ

The special relation that it has to Christ, the Mediator, lends a particular dimension to the church as sacrament of the Trinity, which corresponds to the ways in which the community is referred to the historical mysteries of Christ and to his present glorified state. The trinitarian sacrament is specified therefore by the historical mission of the incarnate Word and the mission of the Spirit that follows on it. This implies that, within the larger sacrament, there is a specific area of symbolic activity that marks out the dependence of the trinitarian community on the mediation of Christ.

In broad terms, this is the area of word and sacraments in the special sense, both of these, evidently, being sacramental in that they are human ways of expressing the Mystery. Both word and sacraments are, in a radical sense, dependent on Christ since they represent, within the general sacrament of the church, the divine saving initiative that is even now being mediated through him. For this reason both word and sacrament, though they come into being within the historical community, are presupposed to the church, just as Christ is presupposed to it. His mediation in favor of the church comes to its fulfilment, not only in the sending of the Spirit to the individual believer, but also in the word received by the faith of the apostles for transmission to later generations and in the sacraments in which the community has recognized the presence of its risen Lord. Clearly, word and sacraments are, in their turn, fulfilled only when the Spirit is sent through them and the divine Trinity dwells in the hearts of believers. Both of them serve the present mediatorial activity of the risen Christ which is fulfilled only in his members.

Saying that word and sacrament, though they come into being within the historical community, are presupposed to the church, raises delicate problems. The word can be observed as it develops through the theologies of the New Testament and through the ongoing history of the church. The development is not normally by way of logical progression; it rather corresponds to the pastoral needs of the community and reflects the insight of its members. Yet, through all this, so long as it is acknowledged by the community and preached in it, it remains the authentic expression of the word of God. By their nature as symbolic activity, less subject to radical change and to intellectual analysis, the sacraments are less at the mercy of historical development than is the word. They can become the subject of dispute, all the more bitter at times because not only ideas but symbols held to be of vital importance are at stake. When it is a question of symbols, the words needed to explain them or defend them against misinterpretation do not always readily spring to mind.

Communities cling to their symbols and are enriched by them in ways that are not immediately reflected on. They can provide sudden flashes of insight when an intuition is seized of how they give meaning to life. St. Paul could be inspired by the simple rites of baptism to sketch out a sweeping vision of the Christian mystery: "You have been taught that when we were baptized in Christ Jesus we were baptized in his death; in other words, when we were baptized we went into the tomb with him and joined him in death, so that as Christ was raised from the dead by the Father's glory, we too might live a new life" (Rom 6:3-4). It is hardly possible to analyze this sort of associative thinking in logical terms; and when the attempt is made, the allusiveness of the existential experience of the symbolism is restricted to what abstract concepts can bear. The same sort of free association, though always within the bounds laid down by the more formal structure of the word, appears in the instructions given in the ancient church to catechumens, perhaps already in the *First Letter of Peter*, but in its most typical form in the homilies of a St. Cyril of Jerusalem and a St. Ambrose of Milan in the fourth century. There was no really systematic attempt made before the twelfth century in the Western church to draw up a full list of seven sacraments. This was precisely because it required a very considerable effort of reflection on the symbolic structure of church life before the community's awareness of the presence within it of the risen Lord could be scrutinized and made the subject of more precise conceptual distinctions.

There was never any hesitation about the Eucharist and baptism; from the first these are recognized as bringing about a mysterious union with the risen Christ that brings the ministry of the word to a certain conclusion, though never one that is definitive. The meaning and ethical consequences of the coming of Christ in person into the eucharistic assembly need to be constantly repeated and developed. Yet it is the conviction that Christ intervenes personally, in a way that goes clearly beyond his constant presence in the community of faith, that makes St. Paul's exploitation of baptismal symbolism something more than poetry; the style is poetic but it reflects the reality of Christ's presence. It is this that will later permit the grouping of both Eucharist and baptism under the general category of "sacrament."

There is not found the same kind of reflection in the early church on its other ritual ways of associating itself with the risen Lord, though there are abundant indications that the community was, as is natural, wedded to such symbolism. Because it clearly grasped its total dependence on Christ and on the Spirit, the church was explicitly aware that its message of divine forgiveness stood under the personal authority of the risen Christ (Jn 20:21-23) and it is this that stands behind whatever forms of reconciliation appear through the later history of the church. The imposition of hands to give the Spirit (Acts 8:17ff; 9:12, 17; 10:6; cf. Heb 6:2) or to impart a special ministry in the service of Christ (Acts 6:6; 13:3; 1 Tim 4:14; 5:22; 2 Tim 1:6) could quite simply not be performed in such a community without explicit understanding that it is the risen Christ who is personally active in these rites.

There are historical developments to be discovered in the way that the ministry evolved into one comprising residential bishops assisted by priests and deacons; but the belief that the ministry itself requires the personal intervention of the risen Christ is bound up with his mission and with the mission he entrusted to his apostles. That the organization of the pastoral ministry led to individual members of the presbyteral college becoming responsible for the Eucharist, while part of the rites of initiation were regularly reserved to the bishop are matters that need to be studied in detail if a full understanding of individual sacraments is to be acquired. None of this alters the truth of faith that the ministry can be given only by Christ and exercised only in his name.

It is only if Christ is tacitly assumed to be a purely historical figure of the past, one who is no longer exercising saving mediation within the church, that the question of the "institution" of the sacraments will be understood in a juridical fashion and the attempt will be made to make its answer depend entirely on historical research. That the sacraments are instituted by Christ is, first of all, a christological statement about his unique mediation. Its historical implications cannot, in every case, be documented by a specific or detailed ordinance given by Christ. Nor will it do to make a verbal distinction between the church as "fundamental sacrament" and its manifestation in the particular sacraments, with the implication that purely historical developments in the liturgy receive "ratification" from Christ. This will not do because the church is the sacrament of the life of the Blessed Trinity and not a continuation of the Incarnation, disposing of an authority that belongs to Christ alone. Where the sacramental life of the church is at the service of Christ the Mediator, it is, for that reason, presupposed to the calling together of the community of believers and, therefore, to the trinitarian sacramentality of the church.

It is a matter for historical research, linked with theological judgment, to decide to what degree the church may legitimately modify its sacramental liturgy; but as to deciding in what manner Christ mediates the life of the Trinity to the community by way of its sacramental rites, that is a matter of discovering what he has chosen to do. Historical inquiry into how the discovery actually came about should be guided by the theological understanding that what is at stake is the way in which the community deepened its understanding of itself as a church gathered together by the risen Christ and the Spirit and celebrating the Eucharist.

The case of marriage is, once again, illuminating. Even as late as the twelfth century, when theological reflection on the sacraments was reaching a consensus that would be officially adopted by the community, there was much hesitation as to whether or not marriage should be understood to be one of them. It was, in fact, only by way of deep reflection on the meaning of the Incarnation itself that the full significance of marriage could come to conscious awareness.

That reflection began already in St. John's insistence on the flesh, a position that would be maintained against all dualistic currents intruding into Christian thought and would find its classic expression, ironically enough given its author's later opinions, in Tertullian's anti-gnostic aphorism, *caro est cardo*: Salvation hinges on the flesh (*On the Resurrection of the Flesh*, 8; Bettenson, *Early*, 144). Acceptance of the sacramentality of marriage was, finally, a recognition of the humanity of the God of salvation; this provided the systematic background for understanding the implications of Christ's calling to mind the original significance of marriage (cf. Mt 19:8). There is the clear indication in the different histories of the sacraments that the community's awareness of the presence of the risen Christ is not the same for all the sacraments. For this reason "sacrament" is not a univocal genus and it is necessary to see, in each case, just how the community understands the term. Everything seems to indicate that the seven should be grouped around the

Eucharist and seen as a system, each one drawing its full significance from the center.

3.3.3 Word and Sacrament

The sacraments grouped around the Eucharist have already been linked with the ministry of the word as belonging with it to the sacrament of the church in that area where it is at the service of the mediation of the risen Christ. Implicit in this is the suggestion that, in spite of their association, there is some kind of difference between word and sacrament. Ecumenical understanding has discredited the distinction between Protestant churches of the word and Catholic churches of the sacrament, but genuine differences of emphasis, and perhaps also of belief, remain so that the question still requires further clarification.

Though it is possible to distinguish a liturgy of the word, where readings and preaching predominate, from strictly sacramental ritual, closer examination reveals that the two merge one into the other. Evidently, the word is still proclaimed throughout the sacramental ceremony even though it takes on there the character of prayer and solemn recitation. Indeed, without the word, received in faith by the community, the sacrament could not take place. Catholic teaching about the intention required of the minister, by which he must intend to do what the church does, means that he must place his words and actions at the disposal of the community; it is the faith of the community that appropriates them and refers them to Christ and to the Spirit. Conversely, it is also true that the liturgy of the word has a sacramental character since it proclaims in human words the mystery of Christ and does so in a language that shares in the power of symbolism. The accepted distinction, which attributes to sacraments in the strict sense the capacity of effecting what they signify, seems to run into difficulties when the efficacy of the word is taken seriously. The early

community was convinced that the preaching of the
message has "a living power among you who believe it"
(1Thess 2:13; cf. 2 Cor 6:7; Eph 6:17; Heb 4:12; etc.).
It is true that the historic opposition of the post-
medieval era between the two forms of ministry may be
partly resolved when the whole life of the church is taken
to be sacramental, the sign and instrument of communion
with the Trinity. Then a common category has been
found for both word and sacrament and their comple-
mentarity is easily acknowledged. This is particularly
significant in the light of the biblical understanding
of the word of God as an active, creative force, and of
contemporary philosophers' insistence on the role of the
word as the medium of communication which provides
the space in which the human person develops. The
question still remains as to whether or not justice is being
done to the Catholic tradition if the discussion is halted
at this point, debate about further refinements being
relegated to the area of theological opinion where faith
is not involved. A theologian's answer to this question
will be in the affirmative if he considers contemporary
analysis of symbolism to hold the key to a definitive
statement of faith in the sacraments, or if he adopts the
more ambiguous attitude that each cultural epoch
dictates the shape that expression of the faith must take
for the church of the age.

There are, however, no easy answers in sacramentology
and certainly not to the question of word and sacrament.
For the moment (the matter will be raised again), it is
sufficient to comment that it is not, on the face of it, likely
that a common denominator formulated exclusively in
terms of an anthropology of symbols will be adequate
to the mystery either of the sacraments or of the word.
To appeal, for example (though we are now at the limits
of what may be called anthropology), to what used to be
said in English linguistic analysis about "performative
statements," which produce results when spoken, and

to offer this as an explanation of sacramental efficacy, is to confuse a possible, albeit not very helpful, analogy with the statement of faith it is supposed to illustrate.

There is a very considerable difficulty inherent in the question of what distinguishes word and sacrament when it is formulated in generic fashion. The fact is that the seven sacraments differ so much among themselves that general statements about them and their relation to the word can hardly fail either to place them on a par with any other public, symbolic activity of the church, including the ministry of the word, or else to claim for all of them characteristics which belong only to some of the sacraments or only to the Eucharist. For this reason generic statements are not likely to prove persuasive because they ignore the different forms that realism—which in this context means the presence or activity of Christ—takes in the sacraments. The only satisfactory way, then, of addressing the question of word and sacrament is to raise it in relation to each of the accepted sacraments and try to see in each case the respective roles of the two ministries.

The crucial case is, not surprisingly, that of the Eucharist. The doctrine of the real presence of the risen Christ affirms something which very clearly goes beyond anything that is attributed to the word of preaching. Yet even here it is noteworthy that the presence of Christ is affirmed in virtue of the plain sense of words, those used by Christ at the Last Supper. Continuity between word and sacrament is apparent here; yet at the same time the sacramental word is believed to possess an efficacy that can come only from God himself. Associated with its recital in the liturgy is the prayer that the Holy Spirit may "come upon these gifts to make them holy, so that they may become for us the body and blood of our Lord, Jesus Christ." It is true that the preaching of the word takes place within this same mystery of the Trinity and that it is directed towards the indwelling of the divine

Persons, just as the Eucharist is. The Eucharist, however, brings into the community of the word the risen Christ himself as the true bread come down from heaven. The transition from word to sacrament is well illustrated in the movement of the sixth chapter of St. John's Gospel. Almost imperceptibly, at first glance, the shift in emphasis is made. At the beginning, word and faith are central, forging the bond with the person of Jesus: "I am the bread of life. He who comes to me will never be hungry; he who believes in me will never thirst" (6:35). Then the realism of the same person in the Eucharist is introduced within the same symbolic structure given by the bread: "If you do not eat the flesh of the Son of Man and drink his blood, you will not have life in you" (6:53); it is the disbelief that the latter provokes that signals the profound change of meaning in the reference to the person of Christ. It is, indeed, a gift of the Spirit, both to be drawn by the Father to believe in the word (cf. v. 44), and to accept the "intolerable language" about the Eucharist (6:60, 63). But that there is a new kind of presence in the Eucharist is not to be disputed; and here is the clearest statement that can be made about the difference between word and the sacrament of the Eucharist. The difference is not to be defined in terms of the community's faith, nor in terms of the general sacramentality of the church. It can be derived only from a totally gratuitous initiative of the Blessed Trinity and of the risen Christ. It is, in fact, only when this unique presence has been acknowledged that it becomes possible to speak adequately of the nature of the community's faith and of the sacramentality of the church, for both are specified by it.

The Eucharist does more than provide this well-defined example of the difference between word and sacrament. It supplies as well the point of reference of the whole sacramental idea. Within it are to be discovered all the elements that belong to sacramental worship as it comprises both the service of God and the sending of the Spirit by the risen Christ. For this reason a general theory of the sacraments must take note of what it is that makes the Eucharist distinctive; to this we turn our attention next. This will open the way for discussing the other sacraments, not in every detail, but in the measure that is necessary for finding a solution to the question of word and sacrament. This, in fact, demands a quite detailed examination of the principal sacraments for it transpires that this question is fundamental. The supposition is being made that when it is resolved it will be possible to state clearly the kind of realism that is involved in sacraments: both the realism that is identified with Christian personalism and the realism that denotes the objective action of Christ. On this basis the attempt may reasonably be made to formulate a general statement about sacramentalism.

CHAPTER FOUR:
EUCHARIST: SACRAMENT OF WORSHIP AND COMMUNION

GENERAL STATEMENTS about the sacraments are often formulated in an abstract definition so innocuously vague that it could be applied to almost any ecclesial activity, including perhaps even the raising of money for the church, as the letters of St. Paul prove in several places. However, if the sacraments are seen, not as individual examples of a common genus, but as a group of church actions related in a special way to the Eucharist, a generic definition will seem to be neither feasible nor desirable. What is needed instead of that is a description of the sacramental system showing how it finds its fullest expression in the Eucharist and how the other sacraments are organically related to that center.

This requires a quite extensive treatment of the Eucharist with a view to bringing into prominence two characteristics that are fully realized in it and are reproduced, in greater or less degree, in the other sacraments, particularly when they are seen in their relation to the Eucharist. These structural characteristics are the worship that is offered in the sacramental system and the communion with Christ and, through him, with the

Blessed Trinity that is brought about in and through worship. These two correspond to the two senses that have been given to the realism of sacramental activity, the realism of personal participation on the side of the faithful, and the realism of presence on the side of Christ. The case of the Eucharist will show that the two are not to be separated.

Because in it Christ himself is believed to be present and active, the Eucharist demonstrates unequivocally the character of gift that belongs to the sacramental system and to the church. In it is given that union with Christ on which all the rest, both the life of the members and the institutional structures of the church, must converge. The Eucharist cannot be deduced from any ideal notion of the church nor from the incarnation of the Word. Yet, once it is accepted as the gratuitous fulfilment of the church on earth, it can be seen as a gracious development of the Incarnation, a harmonious prolongation of the mission of the Word. Only then is it possible to grasp the nature of the church and to understand, in particular, all that is meant when the church is spoken of as the sacrament of the salvation being wrought by the Blessed Trinity through the mediation of Christ.

When the attempt is being made to make the Eucharist meaningful in terms of Christian experience, care must be taken not to fall into the error of defining that experience only in terms of what appears as immediately relevant to the participants. The claim made by the Second Vatican Council that the liturgy, and especially the Eucharist, is the source and summit of the church's activity (cf. *Constitution on Liturgy*, n. 10) should not be lightly dismissed as bearing no relation to pastoral practice. The Eucharist is more than a celebration of the ordinary, even though the ministry of the word cannot ignore the experience of every day. The ritual of the

Eucharist is not necessarily meaningful to all Christians in this immediate way. Personal commitment on the part of the faithful is indispensable; and nevertheless the sacrament itself transcends the word so that pastoral concern is obliged to take note of the initiative taken in the sacrament by Christ himself. If the immediate experience of a community is unprepared to acknowledge what is involved in his presence, then it needs to be opened to it. "Source" and "summit," when applied to the Eucharist, are not metaphors; they are names for Christ and speak of what he does in his community.

For ecumenical reasons the Eucharist is frequently approached in contemporary discussion from the side of sacramental communion since there is very large agreement among the churches as to its significance. The Catholic doctrine, according to which the Eucharist is also a sacrifice, is then introduced as a matter still under discussion. Given the unity of the sacrament, this procedure is legitimate since one aspect does, in fact, imply the other from the Catholic point of view. Nevertheless, if this assumption is not made from the beginning, or if the sacrifical character of the Eucharist is placed in brackets, while attention is directed to communion, it is not at all apparent that justice can be done even to the latter, so much is Catholic understanding of one colored by understanding of the other. It seems preferable, not least for ecumenical reasons, to approach the question from what is admitted by all to be the more difficult side and to enquire what is meant by speaking of the Eucharist as sacrificial. It will be seen that this naturally develops into consideration of sacramental communion as well.

The approach adopted is rendered more complex because there is no clear agreement, even among Catholic theologians, as to what the word sacrifice means when it is applied to the Eucharist. This obliges us to state the matter in its broadest terms and begin with questions concerning the meaning of sacrifice in contexts which are apparently not eucharistic. There is, in fact, reason to believe that some general agreement is possible on these broader questions of usage. If so, the special application of the term to the Eucharist may appear less arbitrary when it is seen to grow out of general Christian principles.

4.1 SPIRITUAL SACRIFICE

In the New Testament's use of sacrificial terms there are two major themes. The terms are applied to Christ's saving act and, more frequently, to the ethical behavior of Christians. These two themes can be analyzed separately but it is of paramount importance for systematic theology that they should never be separated. If they are, the Christian life is reduced to an ethic without its christological context; and, if this happens, the door is closed on any possibility of speaking adequately about the Eucharist. The principle has already been affirmed when it was stated (cf. 2.3 above) that what is said about Christ should not be seen in abstraction from what is said about Christians, and what is said about Christian life can be properly evaluated only when it is related to what is said about Christ.

Since the vocabulary of sacrifice, when it is applied to Christ's saving act, is heavy with allusions to the Jewish liturgy, particularly in the key-text of the *Letter to the Hebrews*, the originality attributed to Christian sacrifice is best discovered in those passages of the New Testament where it is the ethical behavior of those saved by Christ that is spoken of in these terms. Not by chance, the priority given to ethical behavior will assist the interpretation of the specifically cultic language of *Hebrews*.

The *First Letter of Peter*, which treats in particular of the life of the newly baptized, makes free use of sacrificial symbolism. In 2:1-10 several Old Testament themes having a liturgical bearing are combined as images for the Christian life, with little concern for the mutual compatibility of the symbols. The symbol of the temple is set down beside the theme of priesthood and sacrifice and these merge into the concept of the chosen people. In spite of this flurry of images, the sense of the passages comes through clearly: "He is the living stone, rejected by men but chosen by God and precious to him; set yourselves close to him so that you too, the holy priesthood that offers the spiritual sacrifices which Jesus Christ has made acceptable to God, may be living stones making a spiritual house" (vv. 4-5). This is simply an explicitly christological translation of the more direct: "Do not behave in the way that you liked before you learnt the truth; make a habit of obedience: be holy in all you do, since it is the Holy One who has called you, and scripture says: *Be holy, for I am holy*" (1:14-16). Christian sacrifice is stated in terms of its ethical demands which derive from the holiness of God himself. The same understanding is found elsewhere in the New Testament (Rom 12:1-12; 15:15-16; Heb 10:19-25; 12:18—13:16) so that there is no doubt as to the nature of the reality referred to as "spiritual sacrifice."

It is in just the same way that Christ's own sacrifice on Calvary is evaluated in *Hebrews* (chs. 6-10). Applying the words of *Psalm* 40:6-8 to Christ, the author writes: "Notice that he says first *You did not want* what the Law lays down as the things to be offered, that is: *the sacrifices, the oblations, the holocausts and the sacrifices for sin*, and *you took no pleasure* in them; and then he says: *Here I am! I am coming to obey your will*. He is abolishing the first sort to replace it with the second. And this *will* was for us to be made holy by the *offering* of his *body* made once and for all by Jesus Christ" (10:8-10). It is apparent that the key words, applicable to both the sacrifice of Christians and that of Christ, are "holiness," understood as a sharing in God's holiness by moral rectitude, and "obedience" or conformity to God's will.

These are the qualities that make Christian sacrifices acceptable and it is to them that the word "spiritual" refers.

It will already be seen that in the way the New Testament speaks about spiritual sacrifice there is an element of polemic. *Hebrews* is the prime example of this but St. Paul adopts a similar attitude nearly always with regard to the Jewish Law as a whole. It is by contrast with a Jewish liturgy, portrayed as inefficacious ritual, that Christian sacrifice is described as spiritual with the sense, in part, of "sincere." The theme was, however, already one familiar in Jewish prophetic revivalism (Is 1:10-15; Amos 5:21-25; Hos 6:6; Mic 6:6-8; Jer 6:20-21; 7:21-26). It used to be necessary for theologians to insist that neither the prophets nor the New-Testament writers condemned liturgy as such but only formalism in public worship; today the point is no longer in dispute. Even when the prophetic insistence on the prior claim of the oppressed, of widows and orphans, is taken up against a corrupt society, there is a clear understanding that spiritual sacrifice is in no sense a secret religion of the heart. The fantasy that it is no more than that was a product of European romanticism and has nothing to do with the main Judeo-Christian tradition.

Yet even if this no longer creates a problem, and if "spiritual" is given its full sense as meaning "inspired by the Spirit," there is a further difficulty of interpretation. "Inspired by the Spirit" is a reading that serves better than the simple "spiritual" to indicate that Christian sacrifice involves the whole human person and the community; yet just this more precise phrase leads many commentators to propose that the sacrifice it describes is not really a sacrifice at all but that it is called such metaphorically. If this is admitted by a theologian, it is fairly safe to guess that the claim that the Eucharist is sacrificial will later cause him embarrassment. If it does, it is because he has accepted a purely ethical, and therefore in the

Christian context too abstract, understanding of spiritual sacrifice. The source of the confusion lies in the fact that it is the whole life of the Christian, in all its individual variations, that the New Testament calls a sacrifice; and this appears to be so far removed from what is normally designated by the term that its use here, one might spontaneously assume, can only be metaphorical. St. Paul, for example, could see his own missionary activity as priestly, a sacrifice in which he offered up those to whom he brought the Spirit (cf. Rom 15:15-16), and this seems very far from cultic activity in the accepted sense. The question must, therefore, be asked whether the New-Testament writers, when they applied sacrificial terminology in so broad a context, were using simple figures of speech or whether they intended a much more concrete allusion. Their acute consciousness of the all-pervading mystery of Christ would suggest that they did not use such terms so lightly.

The proposal made here is that, when the Christian life is spoken of as spiritual sacrifice, it is being related, whether explicitly or implicitly, to Christ's personal sacrifice on Calvary. Now, this suggestion must be read in the light of the principle, already invoked several times, stating that Christ's saving activity, his sacrifice, as we now may say, should not be considered in isolation from its actual reception by faith, for only when received does it become efficacious. As has been said, this is not to deny the objective status of God's saving intervention in Christ which, to avoid subjectivist misconceptions, needs to be affirmed. But when it is affirmed in an absolute fashion, unrelated to believers, it abstracts from the actual conditions in which salvation is realized.

Applying this principle, we can discern the ultimate reason for calling all Christian activity sacrificial in the fact that it is only in this activity, in all its variety, that Christ's own sacrifice achieves its full stature and saving effect. When this more synthetic view is adopted as a way of going beyond the stage of analysis and of returning to the existential event of salvation, the scriptural use of sacrificial terminology in relation to Christian life will be seen to be quite other than metaphorical. It points, on the contrary, to an intuition into the realism of incorporation into Christ which implies that Christ's sacrifice attains its full dimensions in the community's holiness and obedience to the will of God. Christ is unique as Mediator but what he mediates, it must not be forgotten, is the creative love of God. This love cannot be properly thought of as being received passively for it is given by the Spirit who brings life, life in Christ by which Christ lives in us.

It has been taken for granted up to this that Christ's saving activity may legitimately be called a sacrifice simply because it is an act of holiness and obedience. It still remains to show why this particular way of speaking about his saving activity is meaningful and not simply, in its turn, metaphorical application of a term that properly belongs to a liturgy that Christ's passion and death relegated to oblivion because its time was past.

4.2 THE SACRIFICE OF CHRIST

When the early disciples spoke of Christ's sacrifice they were making use of a liturgical structure of thought which they found ready-made in the religious culture of their time and which they considered significant for interpreting the death of Jesus. As is the case with any such structure of thought brought into service by the disciples, the reality of the mystery of Jesus, him whom they knew as the Risen One, could not be confined within the categories of the Jewish or pagan rites. In spite of this, the images they evoked could express for those familiar with them something of the meaning of what happened in Christ in favor of all. It was, in any case, necessary for the disciples to modify the categories by the very use they made of them. Their authentic Christian sense can be discovered only if these thought-forms are measured against the reality of the Christ-event as it is revealed through the other structures of thought that the disciples were compelled to use.

The *Letter to the Hebrews*, which makes the most sustained use of the sacrificial structure, chose as its model for interpreting the event of Christ the ancient liturgy of the Jewish Day of Atonement, Yom Kippur. Many of the details of the comparison must appear artificial today but the main thrust of the thought is still apparent. The comparison turns on the purpose of the Jewish high priest's annual entry into the inner part of the temple: he "must go in by himself and take the blood to offer for his own faults and the people's" (9:7). He sought God's forgiveness of the common sin; and it is the argument of *Hebrews* that the very fact that the rite had to be repeated every year proves that God has not attached to it his definitive act of pardon.

He nevertheless approved of the rite for it was his way of assuring the cultic purity needed if the liturgy was to be celebrated while the people waited for his final saving act. This has now occurred in the death and resurrection of Christ, the true entry of the High Priest into the sanctuary, through which God pronounces his promised word of forgiveness; for "Christ offered himself as the perfect sacrifice to God through the eternal Spirit" and this, unlike the former sacrifices for sin, "can purify our inner self from dead actions so that we do our service to the living God" in the new liturgy of the heart (9:14). This marks the beginning of a new covenant, given by God to his people, one that the prophet yearned for when he put into the mouth of the Lord the words: "I will put my laws into their hearts and write them on their minds. I will never call their sins to mind" (Jer 31:33-35; Heb 10:12-18). "When all sins have been forgiven," concludes the author of *Hebrews*, "there can be no more sin offerings" (10:18).

Here something very striking has taken place in the formation of Christian vocabulary and it should be kept in mind whenever the word "sacrifice" is used in reference either to Christ or to the Eucharist. "Sacrifice," according to what appears to be its plain meaning, denotes some kind of ritual action performed in the community and directed towards God in the form of intercession, thanksgiving, praise and whatever else may be called worship. It is, on the other hand, perfectly clear that forgiveness of sin requires the initiative of God, not man; this was already understood by the Jewish people before Christ. If, then, it is said that Christ's sacrifice alone brings about the forgiveness of sin, then the word "sacrifice" is being stretched to the limit of its possible signification and certainly far beyond what it signifies in any philosophy of religion or in normal speech. Though Christ goes to his death in the full autonomy of his freedom, the essential feature of this sacrifice is that it is God who is primarily active.

This is more clearly expressed when the New Testament adopts non-sacrificial terminology, as is done in *Romans*, where God's justifying love supplies the theme; so, Rom 5:8: "What proves that God loves us is that Christ died for us while we were still sinners." The most striking expression, since it preserves the language of sacrifice, is that of 2 Cor 2:19: "It is all God's work . . . God in Christ was reconciling the world to himself, not holding men's fault against them." When the center of action is placed in God himself and in his forgiveness of sin, it is much easier to grasp why it has been said that Christ's sacrifice acquires its full dimensions only when the sinner actually receives forgiveness of his sin. The divine act of creative forgiveness and love is realized only when it becomes active through the faith and love and spiritual sacrifice of those who accept Christ's mediation.

Why, if all this is true and if the Christian message is that God himself intervenes to renew his creation, is the terminology of sacrifice preserved? The answer is that, even when God is the principal actor and when we are obliged accordingly to broaden the signification of "sacrifice," the word continues to denote as well the act of human worship offered to God. Obviously, a whole theology is implicit in this simple linguistic fact. The historical evolution which led to the purification of religious ideas in Judaism and in Christianity, while it brought God to the fore as the sole source of forgiveness of sin, did not for that reason eliminate man's role, his instinctive interpretation of sacrifice, his seeking for forgiveness, his repentance, his thanksgiving and praise. All of this, both the divine and the human, is caught up in the single word "sacrifice." Its use reflects the creative quality of God's loving forgiveness which becomes effective, not by what we might imperfectly conceive as God's readiness to overlook our sin or to cover it with the holiness of Christ, but by his creating within us a love like his, however limited it may be by reason of our condition.

The mediation of Christ, incarnate Word, is therefore summed up in a remarkably concise fashion, though perhaps in a word too pregnant with meaning, when it is said to culminate in the sacrifice of the cross. In him the divine creative love first takes human form, in his human love and obedience. In him there is no sin to be forgiven; if he is High Priest, he has no need to offer in his own name the sacrifice of the Day of Atonement. He is rather the one sent to make known to the people that through him the Father's forgiving love is to be given to all. His whole life is dedicated to that mission and to his thankful praise of the Father for it. All that he receives from the Father he returns to him in the Holy Spirit. As the people, generation after generation, accept his mission and, through him, receive forgiveness from the Father, they become part of him so that in him (because he is always the unique Mediator) and with him (because they truly act as persons) they return thankful praise to the Father, borne up by the Spirit of love. This whole history of Christian salvation is concentrated, in chrysalis, as one might say, in his sacrifice of the cross which thereby becomes the source of Christian life and the point of reference for all worship to be offered by those who are saved by it and united to it.

It will be seen that great care must be taken with Christian sacrificial terminology if the mystery of God in Christ is not to be presented in a unilateral fashion. The interpretation will be unbalanced either when the initiative in sacrifice is thought to lie with man, the individual or the community, or when the divine initiative is construed as dispensing with human assimilation and response. This can happen too, though in a more subtle form, when it is not perceived that the human response, even though it requires a fully autonomous activity on the part of the creature, is, as reflection on human freedom shows, a gift of God (cf. 2.1). Because of the divine mystery that surrounds it, the sacrifice of Christ and the Christian's share in it are a living reality that demands radical change in the signification of words such as "victim," "priest" and "offering." These do certainly retain their habitual overtones of religious psychology and therefore quite legitimately evoke those traditional forms of Christian spirituality that cultivate union with Christ in his suffering and death and center on the symbolism of "reparation."

The theologian, at least, should be aware of what is happening here and be ready to suggest ways of opening Christian experience to a broader tradition. Words are being brought into service which belong to a very different understanding of sacrifice than that which is revealed in Christ's relation to his Father. Words such as "propitiation" and "satisfaction" rely on analogies taken from the philosophy of religion that are to be reconciled with the Christian idea of God only when their meaning has been thoroughly modified. They can be justified, as was suggested in Chapter Two, only if they are interpreted in terms of a change that is brought about in man when God's love reaches out to him (cf. 2.3.3.).

Bringing together what has been said about the spiritual sacrifice of Christians and about the sacrifice of Christ, and interpreting both in terms of what was said about Christ's mediation, the suggestion can be made that the sacrifice of Calvary, though it was offered once and for all by Christ and belongs to the past, is not a closed event. Because it was the act of the Mediator it is to be accepted in faith as the creative intervention of the Father in the sinful history of mankind through his incarnate Son. That historical event is closed, though the one who suffered there now lives with the Father. The creative love of the Father is not confined to the past event but continues to be active through the risen Christ, drawing those who receive it into the worship that characterizes Christ at all moments of his existence. To share in Christ's earthly sacrifice is what entry into his worship signifies for his members who are now still on earth.

So, the whole ethical life of Christians is sacrificial, not only because it depends on the mediation of one whose love brought him to suffering and death; but, as well, because it is the service of ideals whose final meaning comes from the fact that they conform to the Father's will and, as such, are inwardly related to the obedience and worship of Christ on the cross. Here, all is the Father's gift and all is subordinated to him. Here Christ's sacrifice achieves its full stature through the Spirit. Into this mystery of the unity of all in Christ enters the mystery of the Eucharist.

4.3 SPIRITUAL SACRIFICE AND THE EUCHARIST

The reason should already be apparent why a metaphorical interpretation of the term "spiritual sacrifice" is inadequate. It would be metaphorical were the Christian message purely ethical in content; but this is not the case since Christian moral action has saving significance only in the measure that it is a sharing in Christ's own response to the Father. In this wider, christological context it is clear that the spiritual sacrifice is, literally though mysteriously, a participation in Christ's sacrifice and, whatever unique kind of linguistic usage this may involve, it is certainly very much more than metaphor. There is, however, more at stake than accurate linguistic analysis, important though that is for understanding theological language. It is a matter of understanding why the writers of the New Testament books could speak so naturally of sacrifice in this way and of grasping that theirs is a christological statement about the Christian life and one that has particular significance for the celebration of that life in the Eucharist.

The transition to the Eucharist is a natural one for the Catholic tradition but, if this sacramental reference is to be fully meaningful, it must be perceived as one that corresponds to the inner dynamism of the Christian life. It cannot be denied that, even within the Catholic tradition, the immediate experience of the faithful is not always ready to cope with official doctrine about the Mass and that it can be seen as an adjunct to Christian life that needs to be justified and assimilated.

If Christian experience is to be the starting-point, then it is in terms of the Christian's dependence on Christ that the opening to the Eucharist must be made. As the term "spiritual sacrifice" indicates, the Christian life should reflect its dependence on Christ's sacrifice both for the reception of the Spirit, without whom there is no Christian life, and for that turning to the Father in worship which is the natural consequence of the gift. The presence of Christ in the Eucharist provides the opportunity to proclaim that total dependence and, in spite of personal failings in following the way of Christ, to do what one can to join in his worship of the Father. The presence of Christ in the Eucharist is no irrelevant article of faith; it is a living presence in which Christ continues the mission of mediator that he has received from the Father. Though he is now reunited with the Father, he remains active in the world through the Eucharist, giving the Spirit who sustains the Christian life and drawing the faithful into his sacrifice. His presence is a real one which corresponds to the original act of mercy by which the Word was made flesh and to the demands of the love that Christ bears for each of those who believe in him. It corresponds to that need for communication and for personal presence that is inseparable from love; but there is more than that, for Christ's is a love that establishes the communication because it gives the Spirit of God.

The symbolic act of eating and drinking, of taking nourishment, in the sense of *John*, ch. 6, opens those who share in it to that fundamental sense of dependence on the love of God that is the heart of the Christian message. The gift is one that calls into life the deepest potentialities of those who receive it so that, without any paradox, to receive is to give in return. This is why the eucharistic presence of Christ as communion merges into the act of sacrifice and again into communion. The christological dimension of the spiritual sacrifice of believers is, when looked at more closely, crystallized into sharing in the Eucharist. The symbols of the Eucharist, both as food and as sacrificial, spell out its characteristics; the real presence of Christ makes it possible.

There is a well-known passage in St. Augustine's *City of God* (Bk. X, ch. 6) that gives a synthesis of the scriptural teaching on the spiritual sacrifice of Christians, bringing out explicitly its latent reference to the Eucharist. Augustine first makes his own the prophetic protest against the ritualism that ignores the ethical demands of God, though he is careful not to define the latter in a way that would exclude from the outset any possibility of justifying ritual worship:

> The true sacrifice is offered in every act which is designed to unite us to God in a holy fellowship, every act, that is, which is directed to that final Good which makes possible our true felicity . . . . The true sacrifices are acts of compassion, whether towards ourselves or towards our neighbors, when they are directed towards God; and acts of compassion are intended to free us from misery and thus to bring us to happiness—which is only attained by that good of which it has been said: "As for me, my true good is to cling to God" (Ps 23:28).

Following a line of thought characteristic of neo-platonism, Augustine moves easily from his ideal definition of true sacrifice to the affirmation that it is realized perfectly in Christ so that his sacrifice is archetypal, that is to say, a concrete event with universal significance. It contains therefore within itself all true sacrifices that will ever be offered by those who belong to Christ. More than this—and here the neo-platonic categories are tacitly adapted to the uniqueness of Christ—this archetypal sacrifice makes other sacrifices possible, for Christ, as man, is Mediator; when he offered himself in his bodily form he was doing it in order that we might be his body. Augustine is going to develop this idea of body, which he understands as an active sharing in Christ's true sacrifice; but first let us see how he reaches that point:

> This being so [see the preceding citation], it immediately follows that the whole redeemed community, that is to say, the congregation and fellowship of the saints, is offered to God as a universal sacrifice, through the great Priest who offered himself in his suffering for us—so that we might be the body of so great a head—under "the form of a servant" (Phil 2:7). For it

was this form he offered, and in this form he was
offered, because it is under this form that he is the
Mediator, in this form he is the Priest, in this form he
is the Sacrifice.

St. Augustine is now in a position to explain why St.
Paul, in *Romans*, 12:1-2, speaks of the life of Christians
as a sacrifice of their own bodies and minds; this is the
"body," namely the Christians, that is offered to God
through Christ; active and passive offering merge here,
with the Christian life being referred first to Christians
themselves, then to Christ:

> Thus the Apostle first exhorts us to offer our bodies
> as a living sacrifice, holy, acceptable to God, as the
> reasonable homage we owe him, and not to be "con-
> formed" to this age, but to be "re-formed" in newness
> of mind to prove what is the will of God—namely what
> is good, what is acceptable to God, what is perfect,
> because we ourselves are that whole sacrifice. [Rom
> 12:3-6a is here cited in full, the key-phrase being:] "We
> are many, but we make up one body in Christ."

Clearly, St. Augustine is using the symbol of "body" as
the theme which unites the spiritual sacrifice of Christians to that of Christ; but this is no mere stylistic device
for he perceives behind the symbolism a real, personal
unity. Brought about by the Spirit, this unity is a dynamic
one because it was initiated in the sacrifice on Calvary
and is being developed now as Christians are in the
process of being re-formed according to their obedience
to the will of God. The "whole" sacrifice was offered by
Christ—but "we ourselves are that whole sacrifice,"
because we are the living body of Christ. The symbolism
of the body now reasserts itself and the entire mystery of
our inclusion in Christ is reformulated in terms of the
Eucharist in which the "body" is offered:

> This is the sacrifice of Christians, who are "many,
> making up one body in Christ." This is the sacrifice

which the Church continually celebrates in the sacrament of the altar, a sacrament well-known to the faithful where it is shown to the Church that she herself is offered in the offering which she presents to God. (Tr., H. Bettenson in *Augustine: City of God*, ed. D. Knowles, Pelican Classics, repr. 1977, pp. 379-380.)

At this point, where the Eucharist is introduced, the difficulty of translating Augustine's neo-platonic thinking into precise terms makes itself felt; some theologians would consider that the attempt should not be made. Subsequent history of the doctrine, however, does not permit us that luxury. The shift of register that Augustine makes, from the spiritual sacrifice with its christological implications to the offering of the Eucharist, is normal for his way of thinking; it can transpose reality into symbol and symbol into a new and broader perception of reality. So, the whole sacrifice, which we as Christians are, is the sacrifice of the "body" already offered on Calvary by Christ, as archetype. But the "body" is offered in the sacrifice of the Eucharist: Christ's body, yes, but that symbolizes ourselves, is our offering of ourselves. The sacrament makes it manifest in its symbols: the church offers herself when she offers the body of Christ.

What St. Augustine is suggesting will be comprehensible to any Christian who cares to think about it and who is prepared to take symbolism seriously, as Augustine did. But the question that was asked by later generations, which had to speak of the sacrament in other cultural situations, was whether St. Augustine's train of thought makes an explicit appeal to the "real presence" of Christ in the Eucharist. Possibly, for those who prefer the suggestiveness of symbols to the logic of rational discourse, the question has no meaning. The understanding that the Eastern Church has of icons is proof that the simple assertion may quite legitimately be made that the holy one who is depicted is present in and through the artist's work; the symbol is not distinct from the reality.

The medieval theologians of the Western Church, who were not notably attracted by symbolism or, if they were, tried to uncover its logical structure, would say about Augustine that he could move from *sacramentum* to *res*, from image to spiritual reality, without making specific reference to the *sacramentum et res*, the objective eucharistic presence of Christ who gives the Spirit. For some of those theologians the ambiguity they thought they discovered in St. Augustine had to be resolved in terms either of pure symbolism or of real presence. As a result, they found themselves in a dilemma, one that has confronted the Western Church ever since.

4.4 SACRAMENTALISM AND REALISM

So long as the debate about the Eucharist remains within the bounds of symbolism and of the faith in Christ which makes its use meaningful, there does not appear to be any real ecumenical difficulty in suggesting that the sacrificial dimension of the sacrament should not be overlooked. Certainly, the Reformers did not object to emphasis being placed on the believer's dependence on Christ and on God; and it is just this that St. Augustine takes to be the presuppposition for, and the correct theological approach to, the claim that the Eucharist is sacrificial. The dissenting churches may not be accustomed to using sacrificial terminology for the liturgical celebration of our union with Christ, but this may simply point to a too rigid separation between ethical practice and liturgy. This can hardly be a matter for lasting dispute so long as the sterile debate about the nature of justification is not revived in its original terms.

There is, however, a real difficulty when the Catholic claim is made that Augustine's symbolic teaching and the scripture on which it is based imply a real presence of Christ which cannot be expressed in categories deriving from any analysis of symbolism. Insistence on this point, which previously had been accepted almost as a matter of Christian common sense since it was incorporated in the liturgical texts, became urgent, first in the theological revival under Charlemagne, then two hundred years later, in the eleventh century, when Berengar, head of the cathedral school of Tours, threw the Western Church into a disarray with his claim that Augustine's teaching could and ought to be interpreted in a purely symbolic way.

Berengar was curiously modern in his cut-and-dried distinction between what is real and what is simply symbolic. If the bread and wine of the Eucharist, he argued, symbolize Christ and our union with him, then that is all there is to be said about it; Christ is present, but in symbol. It was not helpful when his opponents, as they sometimes did, granted his distinction and simply disagreed with his choice of symbolic rather than real presence. It was not easy for a culture that was no longer dominated by neo-platonism to speak of a real presence without interpreting this in terms of material reality and physical presence. It took some time for the medieval church to restore the balance. It could do so only by developing Augustine's theology in terms that he might have found strange and by finding more precise expressions to make explicit what he seemed to take for granted.

From this time on, the only way in which main-line theology could preserve the full mystery of the Eucharist was to make two classes of complementary statements about it, the first symbolic and the second realistic, with each in some way modifying the other. This has created for subsequent theology the constantly recurring problem of how to preserve a balance between the two. The medieval theologians of the classical period, when sacramental theology was first made systematic, paid special attention to the realism of Christ's presence, for the memory of the Berengarian dispute was still fresh;

in spite of this, they gave whole-hearted support to Augustine's symbolic definition of the sacramental order. It was one of the major achievements of St. Thomas Aquinas that he found a way to give a theoretical account of how two sets of statements, seemingly so disparate, could be made about sacraments.

The problem still persists today, for it is not at all easy for any theologian to give adequate attention at the same time to realism and symbolism, the two constituents of sacraments in so far as they refer to the presence of Christ. There are, indeed, some contemporary Catholic theologians who claim to have found a way to leave the old problem behind. The new understanding of symbolism in the human sciences, they argue, makes the age-long theological dilemma a matter of misunderstanding of the terms involved. It may not be quite fair of them if they sometimes illustrate their reference to the "old realistic theory" with the example of the unqualified assertions made by the first opponents of Berengar, for these were quickly recognized in the Middle Ages as an aberration precisely because they ignored the symbolism of the Eucharist. It may well be that they do not mean to be unfair when they give this example and that they are simply betraying their own conception of what the only alternative to symbolism must be.

In any event, no new theory of symbolism, however profound it may be in its description of the human situation, is ever going to be able to account for the way in which the medieval and post-medieval church insisted and insists on the need for an approach to the mystery which is at once symbolic and realistic. This can be put forward with assurance because the statements made affirming the realism of Christ's presence are concerned with the outcome of an action attributed exclusively to God. Since this is so, anthropological constructs based on symbolism are irrelevant at this point unless they are modified in the light of more fundamental judgments concerning the relations which exist between the world and God. This is a matter of such importance that it will be discussed in more detail in Chapter Six. For present purposes it is sufficient to observe that, whatever account they may give of it, Catholic theologians are concerned to defend a real presence and are not satisfied with a purely symbolic explanation which denies it; if purely symbolic explanations are put forward it is in the belief that they somehow can be construed as not denying it.

4.5 THE EUCHARIST AS SACRIFICE

It was at a moment of crisis that the Council of Trent, in its twenty-second session (1562), formulated its precisely-worded defense of the Catholic doctrine concerning the active presence of Christ in the eucharistic sacrifice. The Reformers had rejected as blasphemous and superstitious a teaching that seemed to attribute to the Mass the saving efficacy that belongs to Christ alone. A great deal has been said by historians about the spirit of voluntarism that came to dominate much theological thinking through the fourteenth and fifteenth centuries. It provided a ready-made solution for any theological difficulty by a simple appeal to the will of God, this being held to override any attempt to discover an immanent wisdom in the universe and in salvation, reflecting the ordered wisdom of the divine plan for creation. This could lead, at least in pastoral practice, to extravagant claims being made about the efficacy of the Mass, and the Reformers were not fighting imaginary abuses. Ironically, the Reformers themselves were children of the same age, and voluntarism is nowhere more clearly at work than in their theory of justification, to the degree that imputation to the believer of the merits of Christ was not considered as an act of the *creative* love of God.

The Council of Trent, in its formal condemnations of false teaching, responds directly to excerpts taken from the writings of the Reformers and this inevitably limits the theological scope of these doctrinal "canons." In its explanatory introduction a more positive approach to the Mass was adopted:

> The victim is one and the same, the same now offering by the ministry of priests who then offered himself on the cross, the manner of offering alone being different. The fruits of that bloody sacrifice, it is well understood, are received most abundantly through this unbloody one, so far is the latter from derogating in any way from the former. (Sess. 22, *The Sacrifice of the Mass*, ch. 2; NR 514.)

The words are familiar to theologians; perhaps less attention has been paid to the preceding chapter which places them in a wider soteriological context. Nevertheless, what is typical of the Tridentine approach is that the affirmation of the sacrificial character of the Mass is made in terms of the presence, as priest and victim, of Christ. Not mentioned here are the personal, ethical demands made by the presence of Christ on those who take part in the Mass. This, quite apart from the question of sacrifice, though in fact connected with it, has occasioned a great deal of confusion.

The Council had, of course, fifteen years earlier, in 1547, issued its *Decree on Justification* which had amply detailed its teaching on grace and ethical responsibility. Commentators on Trent, however, when they spoke of the Mass, took their cue from the document of the twenty-second session and so turned their attention almost exclusively to the mystery of Christ's action in the Eucharist. Almost invariably they felt little need to speak of the faithful's part. The French School of the seventeenth century, concerned with seminary education, made the most authentically Christian use of this aspect of Trent's teaching when it developed a spirituality for priests centered on their eucharistic ministry and their union with Christ the Priest. This is itself an indication of the unspoken assumption that guided the post-Tridentine approach.

Even granted the fact that it was Trent, and indirectly the Reformers, who had dictated this line of development, the method normally adopted in accounting for the action of Christ in the Eucharist is open to criticism. It typically took the form of an analysis of a concept of sacrifice which owed more to an incipient philosophy of religion than to an awareness of the unique character of the event of Christ. The innumerable and, it may as well be admitted, baffling "theories of the Mass," elaborated so painstakingly (and, it should not be forgotten, so lovingly) during the course of several hundred years after the Council of Trent, center on different solutions to the question of how the results of such analysis might best be applied to the Eucharist. There was a great deal of literal thinking about all of this, most strikingly in the efforts made to discern the moment and the nature of the eucharistic "immolation" which, it was assumed, had to be found if there was to be a "true sacrifice."

It was a revelation for modern theology when Abbot Ansgar Vonier, a German monk of Buckfast, in his *Key to the Doctrine of the Eucharist* (1925), rediscovered the symbolic dimension of the realism of medieval eucharistic theology. Even he, as will be suggested below, may not have succeeded in pursuing all its implications. His method was novel for the epoch because he had understood that the concept of sacrifice cannot be applied in the same way to other examples of sacrificial rites and to the unique sacramental sacrifice of the risen Christ. His insight, which is evident once stated, needs to be recaptured, if necessary, and preserved.

The experience which prompted the New-Testament writers to use sacrificial categories of Calvary was, in fact, so original that they could display a remarkable freedom in that use. It is the reality of the event, whether that of Calvary or that of the Eucharist, that is paramount; this means that the limits of the analogy of sacrifice must be scrutinized. It may be relied on to illumine an authentic aspect of the mystery; but it must not be forgotten that this will be in terms of ideas that are gained in another, less mysterious order of reality. The event transcends the categories; if we are to try to deal with this transcendence we must correct that partial vision given by one set of concepts by recourse to other, if possible more fundamental, concepts.

There are at least two lessons to be learned from the history of the theology of the Eucharist since the time of Augustine. First, if the real and active presence of Christ is to be placed in its sacramental context, it will be necessary to maintain a balance between statements about symbolism and statements about realism; and, in so far as it is possible, the attempt should be made to coordinate them properly. Second, the post-Tridentine concentration on Christ's eucharistic offering should not be retained as the starting-point. The New Testament teaching on the spiritual sacrifice of the faithful indicates the ecclesial significance of the term "sacrifice" and, for this reason, provides the only profitable approach to the eucharistic sacrifice. It will also, it is hoped, indicate how the statements about Christ, the symbolic and the realistic, are to be coordinated in a coherent system.

So as to remove any suspicion that the Mass is supposed in some way to repeat the sacrifice of Calvary, the celebration of the Eucharist must be clearly placed within that phase of the mystery of Christ in which he who was crucified and has been raised from the dead now sends his Spirit on the community of believers. The eucharistic assembly, in all its particulars, is a gift of the Spirit; and when the assembly celebrates the special eucharistic presence that comes about in its midst, it celebrates the risen Christ who comes only to give the Spirit more abundantly. If we are to discover the implications of this special presence, we must take together the two statements: first, that Christ is really present, and second, that he is present in sacramental form.

It is the second of these statements that points the way to a theological understanding of the first. The sacramental form of the presence is one that is mediated by the symbolism of the bread and wine; because it is mediated by the symbolism it is adapted to the condition of the church on earth. The symbols determine the mode of communication that is established between the church and the glorified Christ and define the role of each. As a consequence, the symbolism, though it is brought into play and maintained by the community, is also open to become the embodiment of the risen Christ who is the same as the Jesus of Nazareth who died on the cross. The symbolic form of a meal celebrates the consummation of the earthly mission of the incarnate Word in heaven and so provides a way for the community to express its own hope of being finally reunited with its Lord in glory. At the same time, however, word and sacrament stress the fact that the community's own consummation lies in the future; they turn the attention of those who still live by faith to that whole drama of earthly existence that brought Christ into his glory, finally by way of suffering and death. In this ambivalence of the symbolism is reflected the dialectic situation of the community and of the individual, for one and all are caught up in the tension that exists between a salvation that is already given and a state of sin, personal and social, from which they are not yet fully liberated. The presence of the risen Christ, it must now be considered, is mediated by this same manifold symbolism. His presence corresponds to the present need of the church.

The glorified Christ becomes present in such a way that the pilgrim church may enter into union with that phase of his mission which preceded his entry into glory.

For this is what the church asks of her Savior, that he should send the Spirit so that she may follow the path he trod. If the church is now called on to offer spiritual sacrifice she needs to unite that sacrifice with the unique sacrifice of Calvary that makes all Christian living possible and that attains its full dimensions only when it is actively shared in by all who are saved by it. All the symbolism of the Mass conspires to channel the spiritual sacrifice of the community towards the event of Calvary. There is an offering priest who presides, symbolizing Christ, the unique priest of the New Testament; there is an offering of bread and wine brought forward by the faithful and raised up by the priest; there is a victim in the sacramental symbol of Christ when the words of institution are spoken for what can be seen on the altar symbolizes the body and the shed blood, which are "for you"; there is a sharing in the victim, representing union with Christ. Let us repeat it, all this belongs to the symbolism of the Eucharist, what the Scholastics called the *sacramentum tantum.*

Because all the elements of the ceremony function as symbols, those that refer to Christ himself quite legitimately represent separately different aspects of his personal activity. On Calvary, priest and victim were one since it was himself that Christ offered to the Father; in the symbolism of the Eucharist, as at the Last Supper, the two are separated. More than this, the symbolism refers to different stages of Christ's mystery, including those which are now irrevocably past, in particular his passion and death and his original victory over death in his own person. In himself, in his own glorified person, Christ is in no way affected by this sacramental ritual in its reference to his past mysteries; he does not die again or rise again. All is done from within the community as it refers back in memory, by way of the concrete symbols, to those earthly mysteries of Christ that provide the pattern for its present pilgrim state. The community, as it follows

Christ, must enter into those earthly mysteries, bringing with it its own spiritual sacrifice. The faithful make up what is lacking from the sufferings of Christ in their own persons.

Does this mean that the real presence of Christ need not be considered, that the sacrifice is one made by the faithful of themselves as they unite themselves in memory with the Christ of Calvary? Certainly, this does describe in psychological terms the framework of the faithful's sharing in the sacrifice of the Eucharist. Clearly also, the community cannot ratify and make its own the sacrifice of Calvary if Christ has not already sent his Spirit on the assembly; and this means that Christ offers in his members in virtue of that mysterious union of the Spirit which identifies them with him even though they retain their own autonomy. The real presence does not radically alter this personal involvement of the faithful. It brings into the space created by the symbolic activity of the worshipping community the glorified Christ himself as he stands in the presence of the Father and offers him the worship that he offered in his earthly existence and continues to offer now.

Already it must be said that the worship of the assembly of believers is united to that of the heavenly Christ who is present in the sacrament. But now, once again, the symbolism that mediates the eucharistic presence must be recalled. There is a celebrant, symbolizing Christ the Priest; there is the sacramental sign on the altar, representing in symbol the death of Christ. It is within this symbolism that Christ becomes present; and the symbolism determines the significance for the community of his presence. The symbolism, now actually mediating his glorified presence, is such that it permits the faithful to join in his present worship in a way that is relevant for them. What is of relevance to the pilgrim church is that it be united, not only with his present act of heavenly mediation, but also with his earthly passion and death, for it must still pass through these experiences. Christ's real presence means that he takes up again his earthly sacrifice, not in his own person, for that is impossible, but as it is now being celebrated and shared in by his members.

In the Eucharist, then, the worship of the glorified Christ is being offered by him because he is present in the sacramental bread and wine. United with his offering is the faithful's offering of themselves which they embody in the same symbols that contain him. The celebrant of the Eucharist, who, after the invocation of the Spirit and the recitation of the words of institution, brings about Christ's presence, continues to symbolize for the community the one Mediator with whose offering the faithful are associating themselves. This symbolic presence of Christ the Priest completes the symbolism of the eucharistic elements; the whole symbolic structure directs the worship of the faithful, in which the celebrant joins, towards union with the past mysteries of Christ and through them with his present worship.

There are certain phrases, traditional for Catholics, which call for explanation. The faithful are said to offer Christ. The language is that of sacrifice in which the community offers a victim. Now, Christ is not present as a victim; he is present in his glorified state. Nevertheless, the symbolism presents him to the faithful, not only as the bread come down from heaven, but equally as the one who was slain on Calvary. It is with reference to his presence as mediated in this second perspective of the symbolism that the faithful are said to offer him. Care must, however, be taken with the phrase if it is not to be understood in a way that would minimize the personalism of the faithful's participation. As St. Augustine remarks, in the quotation already given (cf. 4.3): "This is the sacrifice which the Church continually celebrates in the sacrament of the altar, a sacrament well-known to the faithful where it is shown to the Church that she herself is offered in the offering which she presents to God."

The offering of a victim as a substitute for the community is transformed here, because of the demands of Christian personalism, into an identification of the community with the Christ who offered himself and who must go on offering himself in his members, his "body." Once this is firmly established, Christian faith itself will insist on using the symbolic turn of phrase: we offer Christ; but this will be understood as a confession of total dependence on Christ if we are to offer with him. His offering of himself on Calvary "for us" becomes in the Eucharist his offering of himself "in us."

A second traditional phrase, "Christ offers the Mass," also requires explanation. Here it must be borne in mind that the words "sacrifice," "victim," "offer" and the like, are used analogically with respect to the event of Calvary and even more so with respect to the Eucharist. This means that we should not look for a precise reproduction in those events, as acts of Christ, of a concept of sacrifice developed from other sources. From this point of view, the Eucharist as offered by the faithful corresponds much more closely in its symbolic structure to what is usually described as a sacrifice and to this the text of the liturgy bears witness.

When we turn to the action of Christ in the Eucharist, however, the inadequacy of the terms becomes a crucial point in their interpretation, as was the case with Calvary when it was called a sacrifice (cf. 4.2). The distinction between priest and victim disappears since what Christ offered and offers is himself; now that he is risen, all must be reduced to his love and to his submission to the Father, always in favor of his members. Indeed, since it is the risen Christ who is active in the Eucharist, it is only by straining the sense of the word to the point of near ambiguity that we may speak of his sacrificing at all. As far as he is concerned, in his own person he has entered into the consummation of his sacrifice, untroubled union with his Father. This means that, when Christ is said to offer the Mass, not only in his members but personally, this must be interpreted in terms of the central eucharistic doctrine, that of the real presence.

It seems better at this point to avoid theological subtleties and to follow the instinct of the faithful, affirming quite simply that within the sacramental species Christ himself is present, and adding that this is the Christ who offered himself on Calvary and is now worshipping the Father. In heaven he does not offer sacrifice but he does intercede for his church. This intercession and the divine creative love which inspires it are present in the Eucharist. This is more than adequate to account for the sacrificial term "propitiatory" attached by Trent to the Mass. In the light of the reality that it signifies, the word is being used in a sense which is frankly metaphorical. The Father of Jesus Christ is not propitiated; on the contrary, he is the fount of mercy.

"Christ offers the Mass" is, in fact, a phrase that reflects the interest of post-Tridentine theology. To use the phrase without at the same time relating it to the community's share in his offering is to make a radical abstraction from the actual event of the Eucharist and this does not make for very good theology. This is said without prejudice to the celebration of the Eucharist without a congregation, however much this may appear to be a marginal issue. It is an accepted practice of the Roman Church and is justified because the celebrant, in virtue of his sacramental office, is associated with the whole body of believers.

In a few words, what is being suggested here as an adequate account of the doctrine of the eucharistic sacrifice is as follows. The symbolism of the Eucharist contains the glorious Christ worshipping his Father and unites the faithful's spiritual sacrifice to his worship not

only as he exists now but also as he existed in his passion
and death, since the pilgrim church must pass through for
itself those mysteries which for him are accomplished.

This account, which seems as simple as the event of
the Eucharist warrants, avoids the vagueness of certain
ecumenical discussions which insist on a Jewish and
biblical understanding of the re-presenting memory of
past saving events, especially in the paschal meal. The
latter may serve as an analogy for the Eucharist as it is
experienced in faith; but it is necessary to insist much
more positively on the intervention of the risen Christ.
At the same time the account here offered avoids the
complexity of theories which were current at the time of
the Second Vatican Council, having originated in the
years when the liturgical movement had reawakened
theological interest in the priesthood of the faithful,
understood as a sharing in the priesthood of Christ.

One theory, in particular, which appeared at that time
has here been left aside as too complex (in particular,
because the present writer used to accept it). It involved
the suggestion that the interior worship of Christ, once
expressed by his death on Calvary, is now expressed by the
sacramental separation of the body and blood and that it
is expressed in this way because it is brought to bear on
the eucharistic elements by the intention of the celebrant.
The distinction made between interior and exterior
worship, though it was suggested by the nature of the
case, was perhaps a little mechanistic and human beings
do not really function in that way.

As well as that, it was necessary to call (with Dom
Vonier) on one of the most subtle conclusions of medieval
eucharistic theology, one which affirmed that in the
consecrated bread there is present, formally and directly,
in virtue of the words pronounced over it (*vi verborum*),
the body of Christ; and similarly for the consecrated wine
and the blood of Christ; and this even though the whole
person of Christ is present under each species. Subtleties

such as these may have their limited usefulness in a theology of the mysteries, but they provide an uncertain basis for a theology of the Mass which ought not to be quite out of the reach of the non-specialist. In any case, this whole theory, so it appears now, did not sufficiently consider the analogical character of the term "sacrifice" and so raised problems about the Eucharist to which there is no solution because they are not real problems. It seems better simply to affirm the real presence of the risen Christ, worshipping and giving the Spirit, in the eucharistic bread and wine, and to speak of sacrifice only in terms of the community's worship as it is united to that of Christ.

Because we are speaking of a mystery, of the saving intervention of God in history, a lingering tendency to rationalize the Eucharist always remains; it can manifest itself quite easily in the name of the personalism that is being defended in the present account. Then the attempt is made to confine the mystery within the theologically manageable bounds of Christian ethics. The theologian will protest at what he refers to disparagingly as the multiplication of Masses. The believer, speaking from experience, will claim that a person receives from the Spirit the gift of recognizing Christ in any human situation and of reacting there as Christ would, and that the Eucharist, together with personal and communitary prayer, offers only one occasion among many of entering into union with Christ, and perhaps, if the truth were to be told, not the most compelling. The voice of experience should be heeded; but when, as here, it speaks only in terms of a christocentric ethic, it is not attentive to the fulness of Christ's gift to his church.

The best way, it would seem, to relate the Eucharist in a meaningful fashion to personal experience of the Spirit sent by Christ is to concentrate on the unity of the sacrament. Instead of saying that, as well as communion, it is also sacrifice, and then developing the two trains of thought, the effort should be made to unify these two dimensions of the single sacrament. Christ comes in eucharistic communion in order to give us the Spirit who enables us to join actively in Christ's sacrificial worship of the Father and his giving of himself to the service of a world marked by sin. Though the two aspects are separated in the liturgy, where the canon closes with the "Amen" of the community and the "Our Father" begins the rite of communion, and though the symbolism of the action undergoes a corresponding change, the personal responses required of the Christian in each part merge with one another and should form a unified experience.

Now, the real presence of Christ, as it is mediated through the symbolism of each part of the ceremony, is certainly given in order that the response the Christian makes to his Savior should be intensified and become more deeply personal, for that is the nature of love. Still, there is more to be considered. Just as the presence of Christ is not one that can be accounted for solely by reference to the faith of the community but is a gift of the Spirit, so its significance cannot be reduced to the devotion or commitment of the participants that it inspires. This presence has to do with the irrevocable nature of the Incarnation, with the fact that the Father has sent the person of the Word made flesh as the unique mediator of the new covenant which is established by this merciful act of the Father and which calls for sinful mankind to make its painful way back from sin to living union with the Blessed Trinity. Christian experience is totally dependent on this mission of the Son; it is not yet fully authentic Christian experience if it has not a living awareness of its need to have constant recourse to this Christ who freely offers himself as mediator in the Eucharist.

The Eucharist, then, while it provides a symbolic structure for the expression of the community's faith and commitment to Christ, has this unique quality that it brings the risen Christ into that very same structure so that it becomes an action common to him and to the community. Our faith is in an incarnate Word, pledged to remain with us in his humanity. Even if he is necessarily separated from us because he is risen and we are not, he still comes to meet us in the assembly. Yet the idea of "meeting" Christ in the sacrament, even when it is developed in terms of a philosophy of encounter with all its personalistic significance, is, despite its value, only a resting-place for thought, only one aspect of sacramental experience. It does not do full justice to the mystery, for the person of the incarnate Word, present in the Eucharist, creates the encounter and, as the one who gives the Spirit, evokes himself, with the Father, the response that greets him. He comes as the Savior who brings into being the church, his body.

The philosophy of encounter provides only an analogy, based on human relations, valid for that reason for describing the way in which the Christian should approach the Eucharist. Yet it can prove unequal to the challenge made by the authentic Christian belief that Christ is to be met in any human person because all belong to him and are touched by his salvation. This claim is true; but Christ's sacramental presence brings him into the community as the source of all salvation and this should not be confused with his presence in all those called to be his members. The Catholic tradition has never been concerned to prove that this presence is given to the church; it has accepted the mystery, serenely aware of the presence, and has praised the Father for his gift, knowing instinctively that in it lies the well-spring of the church's existence.

Post-Tridentine theology, because it concentrated its attention on Christ's action, perhaps also because it was not always alert to the analogical character of the use of the term "sacrifice," developed at some length a discussion of the "effects" of the Eucharist. We shall return later to the reason for the choice of this non-personalist terminology, found also elsewhere in the theology of the sacraments (cf. 6.4); in the case of the Eucharist it can be specially misleading. A different emphasis is made when the point of departure becomes the community and its faith and worship.

The presence of Christ, who worships the Father and gives the Spirit in the sacrament, is no longer separated abruptly from the rest of the liturgical action or from the existential situation of the individual participants. The ministry of the word and the prayer of the community move naturally into the sacrament so that, from the side of the community's faith and commitment, the entire liturgical celebration forms a unified experience. The solemn prayers for the coming of the Spirit, spoken over the gifts and over the communicants, put into words the constant theme of the community's worship. In spite of this continuity of experience, there is a reason for speaking in Catholic theology of a "moment" in which Christ, already present in several ways, begins to be present sacramentally (cf. 6.4); and this constitutes the clearest objective distinction that can be made between word and sacrament.

CHAPTER FIVE:
BAPTISM: WORD AND
SACRAMENT

5.1 FAITH AND BAPTISM

THE NEW TESTAMENT leaves no doubt about the close connection uniting the preaching of the word and baptism. "What must we do?", ask those who heard Peter's first proclamation of salvation in Christ. "You must repent," is the answer, "and every one of you must be baptised in the name of Jesus Christ for the forgiveness of your sins, and you will receive the gift of the Holy Spirit" (Acts 2:37-38). This reflects the practice which, from the beginning, has been an essential mark of the Christian community; but discussion about the precise significance of the practice has not reached unanimous conclusions.

Luther's intuition into the saving efficacy of faith alone has undoubtedly left a legacy in Reformed thinking that could still lead a theologian of the stature of Karl Barth to suggest that baptism of water is to be understood as a solemn response of faith, accepting the word of salvation, the baptism of the Spirit; it shows itself also in the recurring debates about infant baptism within the reformed churches. Though his work on baptism came near the end of his life, Barth was undoubtedly still conscious of the heroic days of the Confessing Church in Nazi Germany so that he felt too deeply the pastoral need to make of baptism a firm declaration of public commitment to the Christian community. Yet there is something very close to the heart of the Reform in the naked simplicity of certain phrases in the *Letter to the Romans*: "As we see it, a man is justified by faith, and not by doing something the Law tells him to do" (3:28); or in the exasperation of *Galatians*: "Was it because you practised the Law that you received the Spirit, or because you believed what was preached to you? Are you foolish enough to end in outward observances what you began in the Spirit?" (3:2-3).

On the "Catholic" or sacramental side, where an equal emphasis on faith must be laid, but where baptism is construed as something more than a profession of faith, the problem remains of saying just how it is more, particularly in the case of adults who, by hypothesis, already believe and are justified when they present themselves for baptism. This is, in fact, a problem too for the churches of the Reform. Barth's position was an extreme one and it would probably be hard to find a Protestant theologian today who would not recognize that baptism is both a profession of faith and, in some fashion, an action possessing objective significance for the communication by God of divine salvation.

St. Paul's trenchant defense of faith alone, it should be recalled, always occurs in a polemic context (so in *Romans* and *Galatians*, perhaps also in Phil 3:9), and is directed against judaizing Christians who advocated the retention of the rite of circumcision and the observance of the Mosaic Law in the new community. It is clear, even when he is arguing against this movement, that he sees no opposition between faith and baptism, that, on the contrary, he places them on a seemingly equal footing as far as salvation is concerned. The point is made, within the context of the circumcision controversy: "You are, all of you, sons of God through faith in Christ Jesus. All baptised in Christ, you have all clothed yourself in Christ," so that Jewish distinctiveness is a thing of the past (Gal 3:25-29).

The symbolism of the baptismal rite, with its evocation of, and association with, the death and burial of Christ, is, in fact, made the model and medium of justification: "When a man dies, of course, he has finished with sin" (Rom 6:1-7). In one of his fullest statements he says: "But when the kindness and love of God our saviour for mankind were revealed, it was not because he was concerned with any righteous actions we might have done ourselves; it was for no reason except his own compassion that he saved us, by means of the cleansing water of rebirth and by renewing us with the Holy Spirit which he has so generously poured over us through Jesus Christ our saviour. He did this so that we should be justified by his grace, to become heirs looking forward to inheriting eternal life. This is doctrine you can rely on" (Titus 3:4-8). What all this means is simply that, when St. Paul speaks of faith, he understands it as the faith of one who has been baptized. The center of his theological interest is neither the one nor the other but the Father whose salvation in Christ is brought to us by the gifts of faith and baptism. Baptism is for him the way of entry into the community in which the Mystery is being realized (cf. Eph 1).

There is, nevertheless, a certain priority given to baptism, not as in any way contrasted with faith, but as a rite which in some way encompasses faith, even though it is well understood that faith owes its origin to the ministry of the word. This is bound up with the conviction that faith itself is a gift of God and that this aspect of it is underlined in the rite of baptism. There is, it should be borne in mind, a certain limitation to the key-word of *Romans*, "justification," and consequently to the phrase "justification by faith." The word has a legalistic background and it signifies, in its proper sense, just the opposite of what St. Paul makes it mean in a Christian context. In a system based on a legal code, one is justified by observing the law and this is all there is to justification. Keeping such a situation in mind, St. Paul succeeds in applying its terms to the wholly new situation created by Christ where it is God's mercy, the "justice" of his love, that counts and where sinners, whether Jews or pagans, are "justified through the free gift of his grace" (Rom 3:24). Indeed, it is this new word, "grace," *charis*, that properly expresses the gratuitousness of God's forgiving love. "Justification by faith," an intentionally paradoxical expression, is just one of the images that St. Paul uses when he is trying to put into words the newness of what Christ brings to the sinner. It takes its place beside a series of other images, all having the same purpose, and most of them deriving from the symbolism of baptism in which, without eliminating the personalism expressed in the word "faith," the absolute initiative in salvation is attributed to God. The Christian has been washed (Eph 5:26-27), has been buried with Christ and has risen with him (Rom 6:3ff; Col 2:12), has put on Christ (Gal 3:27), has been incorporated into him (1 Cor 12:13) and into his people (Col 2:11), has become a child of God (Gal 3:26, etc.).

These parallel images not only help to develop the meaning of the more or less polemic term "justification"; they serve as well to show that when St. Paul speaks of faith he is simply turning his attention to one aspect, an essential one because of its relation to the word, of that Christian existence which is formally initiated in baptism and which he elsewhere can speak of as a "new creation" for which Christ alone can be responsible (cf. 2 Cor 5:17). The very fact of submitting to baptism, apart from this being the normal way of publicly professing faith in Christ, brings to light the mystery that salvation in its entirety, and this includes even the faith of the community and of the individual, is a gift from God offered in Christ.

5.2 THE INTERVENTION OF CHRIST

In spite of what has just been said, the fact, of course, remains that faith is, as a human phenomenon, a response to the preaching of the word of God (cf. Rom 10:14-21, where St. Paul is not making a universal statement about faith and its dependence on the preached word but arguing that the Jewish people should have recognized Christ in the preaching of the prophets). Is it to be said, then, that baptism simply provides an occasion for publicly professing the Christian's total dependence on God or that it retains its full significance only when infants, presented in the faith of their parents and of the community, are incorporated into the community of salvation? That it belongs in the category of an initiatory rite is clear, though it is evidently necessary to adapt this analogy, taken from the field of comparative religion, to the unique event of salvation in Christ.

The difficulty, however, does not go away; if union with Christ can be given before baptism, what does baptism add? The question is of even more importance when recast in terms of those who will never receive baptism. The Christian must believe that salvation through Christ is offered to all, whether they are baptized or not; and he will understand this in terms of the divine Word that is expressed in the creation of man and of Christ's sending the Spirit into every human heart that is not closed to God. But, then, what does baptism really accomplish?

The most comprehensive answer to this question should certainly be in terms of the community where the Eucharist is celebrated, into which the baptized are admitted. They are baptized so that they may share in the life of this community and contribute to the sacrament of the Blessed Trinity which is the church and which takes on its most original form in the Eucharist. Baptism itself, in its very performance in the name of the Trinity and as a profession of the community's faith in Christ, looks towards participation in the Eucharist. Indeed, it is only in the Eucharist that the sacrament and the reality of incorporation into Christ are fully actualized (cf. Jn 6:53ff). If this vital relation to the Eucharist is given its full weight, the appeal that is made in the Catholic tradition to a special intervention of Christ in baptism will be set in its proper context of faith. The same risen Christ who unites himself with his community in its central act of worship comes into the community also in order to incorporate those who believe into the assembly of the Eucharist.

How is this entry of Christ to be envisaged? It cannot be legitimate to insist, as did those in the liturgical movement who accepted Dom Odo Casel's "mystery-presence" theory, on the apparent realism of places such as *Romans*, ch. 6, and to go on to assert that the historical death and resurrection of Christ are re-presented and reactualized in the action of baptism. The philosophical difficulties about this kind of telescoping of real events are too great; and, in any case, St. Paul's text is more readily understandable if it is read as an exploitation of the symbolism of the ceremony against the background of belief in the real union that exists between the risen Christ and his members. The "mystery-presence" theory suffered from the difficulties attendant upon transferring into twentieth-century ways of thinking in the West an experience of the realism mediated by symbols that was familiar only to those rooted in the neo-platonic heritage of the Greek Fathers.

The realism attributed to the presence of Christ in baptism by the whole Catholic tradition can be accounted for only if appeal is made to the present reality of the risen Christ and the way he is at work in the world. This was more or less taken for granted in the discussion on the Eucharist where belief in the real presence was accepted as something that is given in Christian experience. The case of baptism, which cannot be explained in the same way as the Eucharist, obliges us to widen our enquiry and to ask ourselves whether the living reality of the risen Christ should not be seen as much more vitally engaged in the life of the church on earth than a theology of the word or even a theology of the Eucharist, taken in isolation, might allow one to suspect.

What is being suggested is perhaps best approached from the description of the Spirit given in baptism as "the pledge of our inheritance," a phrase that leads to baptism itself being called a stamping "with the seal of the Holy Spirit of the Promise" (Eph 1:13-14; cf. 2 Cor 1:22; 5:5). The word "pledge," with its image of a deposit or down-payment, directs attention to the fullness of union with Christ which is to come and whose nature can be formulated only in terms of what we know of Christ's risen state. The sending of the Spirit is directed towards this final and complete re-formation in the likeness of Christ.

Now, this inward dynamism of the gift of the Spirit is not to be explained in exclusively ethical terms, though it evidently entails moral rectitude. It is a movement towards that life already enjoyed by the risen Christ which is "life with God" (Rom 6:8-11; cf. 1 Cor 15:20-28). In some places the New Testament speaks of Christ's present role in this development as the exercise of his lordship (Phil 2:9-11; Rom 14:9; etc.), now that he is "proclaimed Son of God in power through his resurrection from the dead" (Rom 1:4). *Ephesians* and *Colossians* suggest with even greater explicitness that what has happened to the humanity of Christ in the resurrection is spreading outwards in a way, so the images used make us imagine it, that resembles the reanimation of a lifeless body, with the person of Christ as the source of new life. After the hymn of praise to the Father who showers blessings on the community of the baptized, *Ephesians* goes on to speak of the hope for the future that is given to Christians in virtue of the power of God. Already, by his power, God has raised Christ from the dead and has "made him, as the ruler of everything, the head of the church; which is his body, the fullness of him who fills the whole of creation (or, fills all in all)" (1:23). In *Colossians* a similar phrase occurs: "In his body lives the fullness of the divinity, and in him you find your own fulfillment" (2:9; cf. 1:19).

In Pauline theology the resurrection of Christ has cosmic significance. This implies that the Spirit, in which Christ was raised up, is being sent by him, not only to bring about the present and future resurrection of all who belong to him, but also in order to restore the whole of creation. There is vision being presented here of the whole of material creation, with man at its center, being reanimated by the Spirit and being gradually raised up out of the corrupting influence of sin through the influence of the risen Christ (cf. Rom 8:19-25).

There is something being said here about the sheer materiality of the human condition, and therefore of the Incarnation, which is of decisive significance for the whole sacramental order. It draws attention, once again, to the essential truth that the mystery of salvation is no isolated intervention of God designed to rescue man from a hopelessly corrupted environment; that it is, on the contrary, a mystery of communion with the Blessed Trinity which is brought about by the reaffirmation of all that flows from the creative love of that same Trinity. Within this context, what is happening in the sacraments is that Christ, bearer of the Spirit and renewer of creation, is here and now exercising his lordship over the material world.

Here is an aspect of salvation that a ministry confined to the proclamation of the word cannot seize upon in its astonishing newness and unequivocal concreteness.

We can, of course, talk about it, as we are doing now. But if we are to take it seriously, we have to do something about it, actually turn to the materiality of our world in the joyful belief that it is being transformed because the Spirit, who has transformed the humanity of Christ, is being sent through the world to those who believe. Now, this would be a hopelessly utopian vision of materiality were Christians not conscious of the fact that "from the beginning till now the entire creation, as we know, has been groaning in one great act of giving birth; and not only creation, but all of us who possess the first-fruits of the Spirit, we too groan inwardly as we wait for our bodies to be set free" (Rom 8:22-23). But if the humanization of our material environment is a task set before us, the sacraments, as they come from the risen Christ, are spaces for living where the restoration is taking hold in freedom from ambiguity.

This is not a lesson that can be taught, for it cannot be grasped in abstract terms. Personal involvement in living within those spaces is the only way of discovering the message and assimilating the reality. There can be little doubt that the actual experience of the assembly of the Eucharist was a living link for St. Paul between his vision of the risen Christ and his theology of Christ's body, the church (cf. 1 Cor 10:14-22, with the positive evaluation of creation that follows). Living contact with the eucharistic body leads, too, to an awareness, not necessarily reflective, that the humanity of Christ is actively engaged in the restoration of the universe; it has certainly formed the Catholic theological tradition. It is this awareness of the presence of Christ that accounts for the realism of the way in which the tradition speaks of baptism and, indeed of the other sacraments, and of their openness to Christ.

St. Gregory of Nyssa, in a fourth-century instruction, puts it this way:

> The descent into the water, and the threefold immersion, involves another mystery. The method of our

salvation became effectual not so much as a result of
instruction as by the act of him who established a
fellowship with man, bringing life to man by effective
action; so that by means of the flesh which he assumed
and deified everything kindred and related to it may
be saved (*Catechetical Oration*, 35; Bettenson, *Later*,
158).

He goes on to explain the symbolism of baptism in terms
of the way in which it assimilates the catechumen to
Christ in his earthly mysteries; but his justification for
doing so, as was the case with St. Paul, is found in the
person of the incarnate Word; and it is in reference to
him that Gregory can accept the materiality of the water
as well as the instruction of the word. The Greek Fathers
could go farther than this and could even speak quite
naturally of the waters of the Jordan and of the whole
world becoming Spirit-bearing because of their contact
with the body of Christ at his own baptism "when he
imparted some tincture of his divinity to the waters" (St.
Cyril of Jerusalem, *Mystagogic Catecheses*, 3; Bettenson,
Later, 43). Though the imagery was still known in the
West in the Middle Ages, it was taken up into the more
developed sacramentology of that time and made an
expression of the active intervention of the heavenly
Christ in the ceremony of baptism.

In the thirteenth century St. Thomas Aquinas gave
this christological understanding of the sacraments its
classic expression in formulas borrowed from the Aristotelian vocabulary but with a signification radically
modified in the light of the doctrine of creation (cf. 6.4).
He recalls the symbolism of the blood and water flowing
from the side of the crucified Christ, in which the Fathers
saw a reference to the creation of the church (cf. Gen
2:21ff) and to its sacraments (cf. Jn 19:34; Eph 5:31). Then,
after defining the terms of the analogy he is going to use,
he states:

The principal efficient cause of grace is God himself;
in relation to him the humanity of Christ is to be seen

as an instrument united to the divinity, and the sacrament as an instrument that is separated. This implies that saving power is derived from the divinity of Christ, by way of his humanity, even into the sacraments (*Summa theol.*, III, q. 62, a. 5).

No less than the neo-Platonism of the Greek Fathers, the Christian Aristotelianism of a St. Thomas calls for sympathetic reading. Once the technical language has been interpreted in terms of the Christian personalism that inspired it, the witness of the traditional belief in Christ's active entry into the sacraments is manifest, not least because it derives as much from the mysticism of the East as from the intellectual precision of the West.

Before raising the question of what it is that Christ does when he intervenes in baptism, there is already something to be said about the relationship between word and sacrament that emerges once it is accepted that he does intervene. It is now apparent that the sacrament needs to be considered from two points of view. It is, in the first place, a ritual performed in the community of faith and here its continuity with the word is evident, even if the sacrament is seen primarily as a dramatic expression of the believer's response to the word. Seen in this context, the significance of the sacrament can be developed in an endless number of ways.

It is, as some of the Reformers chose to stress, referring to a phrase of St. Augustine, a visible word, replete with allusions to the events of both Old and New Testaments. Its symbolism refers the believer back to the creation of the world and to its redemption in Christ; and psychologists have their own contribution to make in interpreting the symbolism of water. Baptism is a rite of initiation into a community and so may be analyzed in terms of the anthropological and sociological significance of such rites of passage. It is a *sacramentum*, in the sense developed by Tertullian, an oath of fidelity to the way of

Christ, so that the New Testament, whenever it speaks of baptism, places it in the context of moral obligation.

Baptism has, however, a second dimension, one which is certainly in harmony with its symbolism and takes up the symbolism but which, nevertheless, transcends it. This is because the risen Christ is active through the symbolism as the Mediator of salvation, sent by the Father. Because of this active presence of Christ no theological account that restricts itself to the realm of symbolism, however suggestive that account may be in terms of the anthropological function of symbols, and however true, so far as it goes, can be considered adequate to the sacramental mystery of baptism.

The classic phrase used of the sacraments, *significando causant*, in (or by) signifying, they cause, cannot be lifted out of its context in medieval theology and made to masquerade as a prophetic forerunner of modern phenomenological analysis; to pretend that it could is to ignore the evolution that the word "cause" has undergone in the intervening period. The medievals, had they wanted to say of the sacraments "they cause because, and to the degree that, they are symbols," had sufficient command of Latin to say it clearly, and clarity was a tool of their trade. In fact, they used the word "cause" in their sacramentology because that was the term they used to speak of God's creating the world; a St. Thomas used it because he considered that it could be extended to signify as well the active intervention of Christ in the symbolic act of the sacrament; and he went to the trouble of explaining that he was choosing this word so as to make it clear that an exclusively symbolic account of the sacraments does not measure up to the tradition of the Fathers (*Summa theol.*, III, q. 62, a. 1; ib., ad 1).

It is, of course, true that symbolic activity has its own form of efficacy in human personal relationships; it is likewise true that divine providence can make use of this efficacy that is immanent in the world. It might be agreed that this is how he acts when the Scriptures are read and when the word is proclaimed. The presence of Christ in the Eucharist, while it cannot dispense with the efficacy of the word, transcends it. Baptism too transcends it because of an analogous presence of Christ which is better spoken of as an activity since it is not permanent in the way that the eucharistic presence is believed to be. But for what purpose is he present?

5.3 THE ABIDING SACRAMENT

The persistent question returns. To what purpose is the risen Christ held to be active in baptism? The medievals were well advised to formulate this question in terms of the effects to be attributed to the sacrament since this provides the only clue to the nature of this mysterious presence of Christ; but this does not immediately solve the matter. When theologians speak of the effect of baptism they quite naturally adopt and analyze what the New Testament has to say about baptism, namely, to use the briefest expression, that it gives the Spirit. Where infant baptism is the norm, this serves quite well to establish the basic teaching, though it is necessary to explain, with reference to the role of the community and the individual, how it is that the Spirit can be given to an infant. There is, however, a passage in *Acts* that has always exercised the theological ingenuity of the tradition. This is the account of the conversion of Cornelius, his family and his friends (ch. 10).

Already drawn to the Jewish religion and so known as "God-fearing," they are shown to be acceptable to God when, after hearing the gospel, they receive from the Spirit the gifts of tongues and praise; it is then that they are baptized. This was a significant development in the life of the apostolic church, marking the extension of its mission to include the gentiles. Later, the incident

came to give point to the question of the precise significance of baptism since it was accepted that the sanctifying
Spirit had been given apart from the ceremony. When the
duality of soul and body provided a philosophical
background, an explanation could be given in those
terms, as in the baptismal instructions of Cyril of Jerusalem: "The Scripture tells us that, after the grace of
the Spirit had been given, Peter 'commanded them to be
baptized in the name of Jesus Christ'; that after the
regeneration of the soul through their faith, the body also
might share the grace, by means of the water" (*Cata-
cheses*, 4; Bettenson, *Later*, 39-40).

This could, perhaps, be developed in terms of the
incorporation of the believer into the visible church
and this would seem to correspond with the report of the
incident in *Acts*. But, then, does this mean that baptism,
at least in the case of adults, is simply a public rite of
entry into the community, granting admission to the
Eucharist and implying no special intervention on the
part of Christ? The main thrust of the traditional teaching, it will be recalled, envisages Christ's intervention
as his giving of the Spirit. If the gift of the Spirit is not
restricted to the ceremony what is left for Christ to do
in the sacrament?

In theologies which equate the effect of baptism with
the remission of original sin, a rapid answer would be
given to this question and it would be said that baptism
applies to the individual the satisfactory value of the
passion of Christ so that all punishment for sin is remitted, and that this is not available apart from the
sacrament. The legalism of the language reveals that
little attempt is being made to understand in personalistic
terms either the satisfaction of Christ or the undoubtedly
valid concept of punishment; and this kind of approach,
it has already been said, does not do justice to the mystery
of salvation (2.3.3). But, in fact, even the orientation

of the answer misses the point. There is no solution to be found if the question is understood as one which requires an answer in terms of the grace which sanctifies. This is something that St. Augustine was led, by force of circumstances, to perceive.

At the beginning of the fourth century, in the confused situation which followed in Northern Africa on the persecution of Diocletian, dispute arose in Carthage as to the legitimacy of Caecilian in his exercise of episcopal authority, because he had been consecrated by one who had allegedly handed over copies of the Scriptures to the Roman authorities during the persecution, this being considered equivalent to apostasy. It was the whole doctrine of the sacraments that was placed in question by this rejection of Caecilian, for it was inspired, professedly at least, by the belief that the holiness of the church must be shared in by her ministers in their personal lives if the baptisms and ordinations administered by them are to be authentic.

The teaching was condemned at the Council of Arles (314) but was maintained by a schismatic group known as Donatists after its second bishop. In his arguments against the schismatics, St. Augustine did not deny that the ministers of the sacraments should share in the moral holiness of the church; but he did maintain vigorously that the holiness of the sacraments and their saving efficacy do not depend on the holiness of the individual ministers. He argued that the holiness of the sacraments and their saving effect derive from the intervention of Christ himself.

St. Augustine drew practical conclusions from this teaching on the nature of the church and, in doing so, erected a landmark in the understanding of the sacraments. Since the Donatists, by an extraordinary reversal of values, considered the great church to be in schism, and its sacraments without effect, he was obliged to demonstrate that, on the contrary, the sacraments belong to the one church of Christ; and that if they are used by those who place themselves outside this communion they still belong to that same one church, though they will have no saving efficacy because of the sin of schism of those who use them. The pastoral situation, recalls St. Augustine, was similar to that in the African church in the third century, when St. Cyprian had insisted that those returning to the Catholic church from heresy should be baptized since their baptism in heresy could have no validity.

The bishop of Rome at the time had rejected this view of the sacrament, insisting that the practice of the church disallowed rebaptism. The Council of Arles had spoken on this matter also and had made the doctrine more precise by declaring that baptism administered by heretics was to be regarded as valid if they accepted the doctrine of the Trinity. Augustine now goes further, giving the reason why rebaptism is not permitted; it is here that he proposes a refinement of sacramental theology that is accepted by the whole subsequent tradition:

> The reason why the blessed Cyprian and other eminent Christians . . . decided that Christ's baptism could not exist among heretics or schismatics was that they failed to distinguish between the sacrament and the efficacy or working out of a sacrament. Because the efficacy and working out of baptism, in freedom from sins and in integrity of heart, was not found among heretics, it was supposed that the sacrament itself did not exist there. But if we turn our eyes to the multitude within the fold, it is clear that those within the unity of the Church who are perverse and lead wicked lives can neither give nor have the remission of sins. Nevertheless the pastors of the Catholic Church spread through the whole world were quite clear that such men had the sacrament of baptism and could

confer it; and through them the original custom was afterwards established by the authority of a plenary council. Even when a wandering sheep has received the Lord's brand-mark at the hands of dishonest robbers, and then comes into the security of Christian unity, it is restored, freed, and healed; but the Lord's brand-mark is recognized, not disallowed (*On Baptism, against the Donatists*, 6:1; Bettenson, *Later*, 241).

St. Augustine agrees with St. Cyprian, and for that matter with the Donatists, that baptism administered within a schismatic or heretical sect cannot have saving efficacy; nevertheless, assuming that those who adhere to such a sect have administered a genuine sacrament (certain types of heresy could prevent this, but not simple schism), the sacrament cannot be repeated if the one who received it should return to the community of the church. He has truly been baptized and, even while the sin of separation remains, this creates a situation which Augustine illustrates by the image of the brand-mark carried by a sheep.

The key to Augustine's explanation of the church's refusal to rebaptize is found in the crucial distinction between the "sacrament" and the "working out of the sacrament" in the forgiveness of sin and the giving of the Spirit for the personal sanctification of the individual. In juridically-oriented sacramentology this distinction was represented as one between a "valid" and a "fruitful" sacrament; but St. Augustine was not speaking that kind of language; his distinction is based on his understanding of the nature of the church, as it depends on Christ and as it is actually realized in a sinful world. The fact that the church refuses to repeat the sacrament of baptism—and the argument applies also to orders—means that the sacrament is not just a passing ceremony intended to confer the Spirit of sanctification. Because it is a sacrament belonging to Christ it is something that endures, something that is, in itself, independent of the changing personal relation of the one who bears it to the community and to Christ.

The notion of an abiding sacrament is thus introduced into Catholic teaching. It was not a pure invention on the part of Augustine; he simply put into words the implications of a practice that the church had maintained even in the face of adverse criticism made in the name of the holiness of the church. It would be pointless to press St. Augustine's text, and in particular the metaphor of brand-mark, so as to make them yield the later, precise doctrine of an indelible character. Nevertheless, it is quite easy to recognize the historical continuity between the two moments of theological development, not least because the medieval proponents of the character make explicit reference to Augustine's teaching. Certainly, the broad context of Augustine's solution should not be lost from view. If it is, the more developed medieval theory and doctrine can look as though they were nothing more than a piece of unwarranted speculation.

Augustine adopted without question the fundamental intuition of St. Cyprian's ecclesiology according to which the one, true church is the unique dwelling-place of the Holy Spirit; and theirs was no idealistic image of the church. They meant the sociologically determinable entity formed by the communion of local churches with a united episcopacy. The Spirit is given, this is their common position, only to those who are in communion with the one visible church. Yet the sacraments, St. Augustine goes on to specify, must be held to be truly exercised outside the bounds of the church. The reason is that they are sustained by Christ himself who, through them, continues his saving mission to the church. Because they are his sacraments, they transcend the personal unworthiness of those ministers who have maliciously separated themselves from the church. Those who, with similar maliciousness, adhere to sectarian ministers cannot hope to receive the saving effect of baptism; yet they do receive the authentic sacrament, sustained by Christ, and this may never be repeated.

If they return to communion with the church they will then receive the Spirit who dwells only there, and then the implications of the abiding sacrament they carry in their persons will be fulfilled. It is not necessary to remark that St. Augustine's unqualified denial that the Spirit can be received by those not in communion with the one church was based on the supposition, which he took to be evident in the case of the Donatists, that the schism was perversely wrong-headed. It is, however, an integral part of his theology, as it was of Cyprian's, that true sacraments, precisely because they are sustained by Christ, pertain to the one, visible church.

There seems little doubt that, for Augustine, the giving of the Spirit is linked, not so much with the abiding sacrament as with entry into the communion of the church. Once the communion of charity was restored through reconciliation, the reality corresponded to the sacrament. Later theologians, having lost sight of Augustine's sacramento-realist understanding of the church, sometimes envisaged the abiding sacrament as a sort of invisible reduplication of the visible sacramental ceremony. Then they were led to formulate complex hypotheses about how this abiding sacrament was involved in giving the Spirit when the baptized schismatic returned to the church. St. Augustine's thesis is much more simple. As far as sacramentality is concerned, the person baptized in schism already belongs to Christ and therefore to the church, even though his separation from the church introduces a breach into its communitary sacramentality. What is required is that visible communion be restored and that the reality of the bond of true charity correspond to the restored sacramental unity. This suggests, though St. Augustine does not pursue the matter, that the abiding sacrament should be conceived, not in the static way that the image of "brand-mark" or "character" might appear to indicate, but as a dynamic insertion into the sacramentality of the church and one that is given by the risen Christ himself.

The word "dynamic" is used to signify, first of all, that the abiding sacrament of baptism, because it holds the one who bears it in a lasting relationship with Christ, imposes a constant obligation that the reality of that person's life should correspond to this sacramental incorporation into Christ. This moral exigency implies a further dynamism in the abiding sacrament, this time corresponding to the sacramentality of the community which is given its fullest expression in the Eucharist. If the abiding sacrament incorporates a person into the sacramentality of the church, then that person should be a sacrament of the Trinity, as the church is, and that person is invited to join the community in the Eucharist, the sacrament of Christ the Mediator of the life of the Trinity.

The presence of Christ in the Eucharist, with all that implies, needs to be taken into account when we attempt to say what it is that baptism gives, just as it needs to be taken into account when we define the nature of the church. If baptism incorporates into Christ, this is achieved in that sacramento-realist way that corresponds to the nature of the church on earth. The realism is the personal response to Christ that is the gift of the Spirit. The sacramental aspect is given by the abiding sacrament or character which is directed towards participation in the Eucharist. This implies that the meaning of the character must be thought out in terms of the Eucharist and the special form of union it affords between the church on earth and the risen Christ.

The whole "spiritual sacrifice" of the faithful can be incorporated into the eucharistic worship of the risen

Christ only because of the baptismal character. It would be a mistake to dismiss this capacity for sacramental union with the risen Christ, which is unique, by referring to a juridical analogy and saying that it consists in the right and duty of taking part in the Eucharist and the other sacraments. Juridical categories are hopelessly inadequate in sacramental theology which has to deal with community actions whose symbolism is transformed by the intervention of Christ. He makes what began as manifestations of the faith of the assembly living embodiments of his own person and of his own action. What was simple liturgy of the people is now drawn into the mystery of the divine, creative Word, incarnate in Christ and now worshipping the Father in glory and sending the Spirit on his church. It is this creative Word in his humanity who is active in the Eucharist and in baptism.

In baptism he sends the Spirit to transform the whole person of the believer; he also incorporates the believer into his sacramental body through which he has chosen to be active. The sacramental incorporation, because it comes from the creative Word and because it is in view of the creative Word's presence in the sacraments, can hardly be thought of as other than a real, though partial, assimilation of the baptized person to the person of the risen Christ. This view needs to be completed by discussion of the character of orders which enables the person who bears it to represent the risen Christ within the community (cf. 8.1.2). But, if this is taken for granted at present, and if the presence of the risen Christ is taken as assured in the assembly, then the baptized person's assimilation to the risen Christ is his capacity to share in that action of Christ, to enter into his sacramental worship and to be sanctified in it.

Going beyond the letter of the text, which could be adequately interpreted in terms of the rite of baptism and the Spirit it imparts, a long tradition has seen a reference to the character in the words of St. Paul: "You have been stamped with the seal of the Holy Spirit of the Promise" (Eph 1:13; cf. 4:30). The character is, in fact, the seal of the risen Christ, imparted by the Spirit, which gives those who receive it a gift that falls within the logic of the Incarnation, the possibility of joining with Christ in his sacramental worship.

If the church is the sacrament of the Blessed Trinity, and if it is animated by the indwelling of that Trinity, the character, in its specific function, relates the person who bears it to the Person of the Son in his mission as mediator between the church and the Trinity. It is for this reason that St. Thomas Aquinas, with an intuition that he did not fully develop, spoke of all the characters (of baptism, confirmation and orders) as ways of sharing in the priesthood of Christ (*Summa theol.*, III, q. 63, a. 3). He clearly had the Eucharist in mind when he said this. His insight may be preserved if we follow his own proposal that the priesthood of Christ (discussed in III, q. 22) along with his other roles be subsumed under the general office of mediator (III, q. 26). This will allow greater flexibility in adapting his way of thinking to a more developed theology of the church (cf. 8.1.3).

The Eucharist shows the church of the word brought beyond the word into a union with the incarnate Word that is surpassed only in the vision of God which comes at the end of earthly existence. The word that the church preaches can, by the power of the Spirit, implant faith and love in the hearts of those who hear it and it is in this way that the Blessed Trinity comes to dwell with them. When those who are brought to faith by the preaching of the word receive baptism they confess their belief publicly and are received by the community of believers. It is then that they become fully incorporated into Christ—both mentally and sacramentally, as St. Augustine liked to put it.

When word gives place to sacrament it is the risen Christ himself who marks the difference as he brings

138 *Baptism: Word and Sacrament*

the believer into the sphere of the Eucharist. Those who already belong to the community of the Eucharist and who receive the new candidate for admission are not able of themselves to create a new participant in that sacrament which is Christ's. He must intervene himself in the rite of initiation and set his seal on the one whom the church presents. The seal is given only in baptism. The mystery of salvation, which is universal and which is at work in countless ways, is crystallized in baptism and becomes a call to personal sharing in the Eucharist.

CHAPTER SIX:
THE QUESTION OF REALISM

6.1 THE RETREAT FROM REALISM

THE ACCOUNT ALREADY GIVEN of the relationship between word and sacrament in the cases of the two principal sacraments has drawn on ideas concerning the presence and activity of the risen Christ that not all contemporary theologians are willing to employ. The reasons for their reluctance are many. It is understandable that non-Catholic traditions, however much they may display an increasing openness to the sacramental idea, will be inclined to subordinate it to their intuition concerning the paramount efficacy of the word. But in Catholic theology too the post-conciliar years have revealed a marked disinclination on the part of some theologians to speak in a direct fashion of an intervention of Christ in the sacraments which would, if its meaning were to be pressed, transcend the category of word. Their over-riding concern is to present the traditional doctrine of the sacraments in a way that will not involve the introduction of manners of speaking that they believe to be incomprehensible today.

As a consequence, certain discussions of the sacraments in contemporary Catholic writing—one thinks of what might be called Parisian theology, the name indicating less a geographical than a spiritual homeland—are appendages to sometimes subtle developments of new categories drawn from the human sciences. For the most part, interest is shown in research into the psychological and sociological functions of symbolism, interpreted according to one or other of the post-Kantian theories of knowledge. All of this is very sophisticated and, in the nature of things, addressed to a small circle of initiates. Such influence as it has had on pastors and teachers of religion has made itself felt in publications that direct attention to the human and, in particular, the communitary significance of the sacraments, and attempt to express in those terms their christological dimension.

In the sphere where German theology is dominant, the grandiose intuitions of idealism are still at work, the style being already familiar to the English-speaking world in the writings of Paul Tillich. When taken up by Catholic theologians the influence of idealism will betray itself, for example, in the use of the word "objectivize." The sacraments are, typically, seen as the "objectivization" of the mystery of salvation in the community of the church. This means that the Holy Spirit, who has expressed himself in definitive fashion in the person of Jesus Christ, is now in process of integrating believers into that archetypal achievement, and that he does this most forcefully when the church expresses in ritual its deepest reality as the community of Christ. The ritual corresponds to the most significant moments in the life of the human community and its individual members, and inserts those moments and all that they represent into that vast movement of the Spirit which will finally transform all creation into the likeness of Christ. The poetry of idealism makes its account of the sacraments more accessible than the intellectualism of the French discussions so that its influence is quite widespread. Where the two streams meet is in their agreement that any valid approach to the sacraments must place man and his community at the center, though, of the two, the account inspired by idealism is more open to talk about divine intervention in the sacraments.

As far as the demand for developing the human side of sacrament goes, there is every reason to applaud the orientation of these theologies. However, sacramentology and liturgy cannot be treated as though they were independent theological disciplines to be developed in unquestioning alliance with the human sciences associated with the philosophy of religion. Theologians in the idealist tradition have the merit of realizing this and, however much one may disagree with the philosophy underlying their sacramentology, they do make it apparent that this part of theology can be developed only in the form of a synthesis of all the topics of systematic theology. This is hardly surprising since sacraments are concrete existential events in which all the things theologians talk about converge in lived experience.

It is particularly hazardous for someone trying to be a theologian to make use of the human sciences in order to lead theology into new fields of experience if he is not already competent in the whole of systematic theology. He could end up as a dilettante in the human sciences and outside theology altogether because he has not mastered the method of either. When it comes to speaking about divine intervention in the sacraments, the fundamental question is not one of the phenomenology of symbolism. Such an approach, because of the categories it employs and the point of view it adopts, systematically excludes, as a matter of method, any consideration, either for or against, of the action of God. It may consider the believer's conviction that, as a member of a community, he experiences God's saving help; but this is not at all the same thing as making statements about God which can be shown to be meaningful and are affirmed as true.

The crucial question of sacramental theology, whether or not Christ is present and active in the church's symbolic acts, cannot, in fact, be decided by any theology; it is already a matter of faith. What is a matter for theology is the meaningful account that can be given of the real presence and activity witnessed to in the Catholic tradition. There are some theological projects which are incapable of dealing with this as adequately as the Catholic tradition requires. The reason is that their authors, either explicitly or implicitly, have decided that it is for them a matter of intellectual honesty to exclude the possibility of all talk about God's objective way of acting in the world. This can be decided implicitly if it does not occur to someone that there is a problem and that, simply by not referring to God's action in the sacraments, one has retreated from the realism of the Catholic tradition.

6.2 THEOLOGY AND A METAPHYSICS OF THE REAL

The retreat from realism is sounded in its most unmistakable form when a theologian announces that he is going to dispense with metaphysics because modern man does not think metaphysically. This is, of course, a very metaphysical statement on his part since it involves, apart from the non-inductive sociology, at least a negative judgment on man's capacity to know the real. When made with the seriousness it calls for, such a judgment represents a respectable philosophical option, but it is one that severely limits those who are trying to develop the doctrine of the Bible. The books of the Bible were written by people who took it for granted that man's salvation comes only from God and that it is possible to communicate this message to others. Unless we are willing to say that these writers were using a code in which the word "God"—Yahweh, the Lord, the Father—whenever it occurs as the subject of a sentence, stands for "I feel that God," we shall have to make use of metaphysics in systematic theology.

It will not do to use the pseudo-metaphysics that some contemporary theological writers portray in caricature so as to facilitate their rejection of it. The metaphysics needed is one that will justify the judgment of a reader of the Scriptures who, having taken due note of all that needs to be said about literary forms, still considers that the text is speaking about an objective action of God in history, though obviously, one that achieves its purpose only when it has been accepted and acted upon by human persons.

Since a matter of such urgency as this can hardly have been left to the outcome of a dialogue between the individual reader and the scripture-scholars whose work he is familiar with, it has to be assumed that the community of believers is the principal interpreter of the New Testament. The Catholic community, which over the centuries has been at some pains to work out the implications of its role as interpreter, accepts that certain normative readings of the Scripture are guaranteed by the Holy Spirit. The teaching authority of the church, if its role is to be incorporated into the method of scientific theology, functions as a certifier of the central data of the science which, in the case, are made up of specific ways of reading passages of the Scripture which are held to be of essential importance to the community's way of life. An example, which directly concerns the sacraments, is the reading given in the Catholic tradition to the words, "This is my body." Of all the many interpretations which have been given, or could be given, of these words, some of them mutually incompatible, some of them not, this tradition has insisted that the word "is" must be given its strong existential sense, the one that it has in a judgment about an objective state of affairs. There is no developed theology involved in this insistence; in this lies its force. Nevertheless, only a theology equipped to deal with the word "is," used in the sense indicated, is able to integrate this conviction of the community into its systematic thinking.

Now, metaphysics, in its only authentic form—and this is all that the magical word means—deals with what is meant by the word "is," and it is primarily interested in those events where people use the word in its strongest possible sense. This is what distinguishes metaphysics from all other sciences, for all the others operate on particular aspects of reality that can be formulated in ideas, in abstract concepts, whereas metaphysics grapples with the only non-abstract reality there is, the individual person or thing, the concrete existant, and it tries to say why it is that we use the word "is" when we speak about that reality. This may sound simple and, in fact, if one goes the right way about it, it is simplicity itself. But a word of warning is called for: metaphysics is a difficult science to handle because, if we are not constantly on the alert, we are going to substitute for the reality we are supposed to be concentrating our attention on, something else; and if it is something else, it is no longer reality. It may seem odd that this should happen, but the history of philosophy shows that it happens all the time. The reason is that, once people start thinking about what "is," they are obliged to introduce into their thinking abstract concepts, just as much as are the practitioners of other sciences. The need to refine these concepts and reshape them and then the interplay among the concepts can become so absorbing that the concepts can imperceptibly impose themselves as the object of the whole enterprise. The concepts and the problems they raise because of their necessarily fragmentary grasp of reality become the only theme; when that happens, whatever it is that the thinker is doing, it is certainly not metaphysics.

Then the starting-point, the true object being studied, the really existant which "is," is lost from sight. The enterprise goes on but it is now pseudo-metaphysics, that is, thinking about thinking, not about the irreducible fact of reality. The would-be metaphysician finds himself in the preposterous position of constructing ever more complex theories by which he can think himself back to the real, to what "is." Of course he will not succeed in doing so, for he has had the last sight of the real he is going to have at his starting-point, the one that he, along with other ordinary people, takes for granted when he is not immersed in his theories. When the real is lost sight of in systematic thinking, the "is" of existential judgments can come to mean all sorts of things except the one thing only it can mean, the knowing subject's acknowledgment of the originality of the other, the acceptance of the objectively true.

When we speak of authentic metaphysics, we mean one that is constantly aware of this originality or givenness of existence, no matter how complex the thinking about it becomes. Without the kind of openness to the radical newness of each concrete event that only authentic metaphysics can preserve, systematic theology finds itself enclosed within the limitations of whatever scheme of concepts it is that the individual has adopted as his own. Now, a scheme of concepts—for no other reason than that it is a scheme of *concepts*—is quite simply incapable of grasping what is meant by the strongly existential signification of the word "is." By definition, then, it is incapable of dealing with the formal point of the Catholic tradition's reading of statements such as: "You *are* the Christ, the Son of the living God" or "This *is* my body." According to this reading, these statements make judgments about reality. Though judgments obviously employ concepts, they transcend them and their necessarily limited content. They transcend them because the person who makes such judgments is letting it be known that he is talking about an objective state of affairs, however much he may be prepared to admit that his conceptual grasp of it requires further development. Other people know that this is what he is talking about, even if they may, for their part, make a different judgment about the objective state of affairs. Existential judgments which are the currency of our habitual openness to reality are rooted in immediate sensible experience, in what we hear, see with our own eyes, touch with our own hands.

Existential judgments of faith are not of this kind. They differ, firstly, because we rely on the community's assurance that certain apparently existential judgments that are found in the Scriptures are, indeed, to be understood to use the verb "to be" in its strong existential sense. They differ also because it is the Holy Spirit, acting through the believer's faith, who gives him contact with the reality of God and with his actions in the world and so enables him to make his own the judgments proposed by the community. Such faith-judgments are an invitation to theological thinking; but the contact with divine reality that they give and the objective statements that they permit regarding Christ or the Eucharist, these are prior to theological thinking and constitute its presuppositions. If a Catholic theologian chooses to ignore them or if he is still under the sway of the Cartesian "methodic doubt" about them, he quite literally renounces the only contact he can have, at least in his theology, with the reality he hopes to talk about.

Failure to distinguish between faith as involving existential judgments and faith as using concepts marks a very large part of post-conciliar theology. The project has been announced of reformulating the faith in ways that will make it more understandable to people of today. This was always the task of the systematic theologian, however well or badly he may have fulfilled it. What needs to be grasped, both by theologians and those who are exposed to their thinking, is that this quite legitimate project of reformulation is almost exclusively concerned with *concepts* or with developed schemes of concepts.

Whether new concepts are adequate or not is something that can be decided only after they have been tried out and discussed. All of this leaves untouched the formal signification of those judgments of faith which the tradition affirms in the strongly existential sense. There really is no way of reformulating the Council of Chalcedon's affirmation that our Lord Jesus Christ "is one and the same" as the divine Son, whatever effort needs to be put into translating the concepts "person" and "nature" that the council used when taking position in reference to the contemporary dispute, and however much it may be necessary to think about the mystery of God and its significance for man that are implied in the affirmation. For just the same reason it is not possible to find a new way of expressing the "is" of "This is my body."

Theologians, because their whole training equips them to deal with concepts, can lose their bearings very easily in matters of Catholic faith if they allow themselves to slip unawares into thinking that concepts have the last word. A telling symptom of this malaise is found in the current popularity of theological "models"—they are proposed for the Incarnation, for the church, for the sacraments, even for God. They betray the hypnotic fascination that conceptualism has for theologians for, if concepts are all that count, the theologian shows a fitting modesty when he presents his own conceptual scheme as one possible way among many of looking at things. The term "model" is, of course, borrowed from sub-atomic physics where it designates a theoretical construct, a piece of imaginative thinking, which, for the moment at least, serves to link in a meaningful pattern a series of phenomena affecting the measuring instruments used in experiments. Such a construct or model is considered useful so long as it permits a physicist to predict with probability the outcome of further measurement; and several different models may be maintained concurrently because (so it would seem) different forms of measurement are used. In all of this the physicist is making no claim to know by means of his model how things really are; he would probably say that such a claim would be meaningless since his method does not consider that sort of thing. A similar suspension of judgment about how things really are seems to attach itself to the transferred use of the model-idea in theology. Models are temporary hypotheses, always reformable, and offer a useful way of accounting for all the variations that have occurred and still occur in Christian theology.

There is no need to quarrel with this way of presenting the task of theology if it is agreed that "models" are constructed by schemes of interlocking concepts which may legitimately be proposed for discussion as ways of presenting the conceptual content of the faith. But the method of physics is not the method of theology. Theology presupposes a true knowledge about God, given in the judgments of faith, which the physicist certainly does not lay claim to in respect of his object of study. This is something the theologian must come to terms with and account for. So long as he restricts his investigations to concepts he has no chance of accounting for the claim made for faith that it gives true knowledge about God's objective act of salvation. There is no way out of the dilemma of conceptualism except the one that has always been given: the rediscovery of existence.

The community of believers can take the truth of faith for granted; the theologian must justify that; and the kind of metaphysical thinking needed for justifying the claim the church makes about the possibilities of human knowledge, is needed too for the whole theological project. What this comes to is that there is a general hermeneutic which ought to be common to all theologians of the Catholic tradition; which transcends legitimate differences of conceptualization; and which is presupposed to all discussion of inter-subjectivity or other relationality. This is not a hermeneutic (a method for reading a text) that consciously involves methods of literary analysis; it is given in the person who, as he reads, is open to being, to the act of existence, to God himself and to his saving action. Existence is the first and constant gift of the Creator and we can seize it, or be seized by it, only in the act of judgment. In the act of faith, it is God's own existence and his saving action that seize us and impose on us their own irreducible objectivity. These are thoughts we must keep in mind and apply as we turn again to the question of word and sacrament.

6.3 WORD AND SACRAMENT

It may seem that the discussion has strayed far away from the question of the relationship between word and sacrament. In fact the return to basic principles was necessary. Answers to particular theological questions always involve the fundamental philosophical options of theologians so that it is impossible to understand why they reply as they do if we do not go back to what they have to say, or what they assume, about God and our possibility of making any meaningful and true statement about his action in the world.

The preceding chapters contain the proposal that the Eucharist and baptism, in spite of their integration into the ministry of the word, are to be distinguished from it by reason of the unique form of presence adopted in them by the risen Christ. It is just this kind of presence, distinct from whatever kind of presence Christ may be said to have in the word of preaching or in the assembly of the faithful, that many contemporary theologians are reluctant to speak about. They are, in fact, obliged to impose such silence on themselves once they have chosen to conduct their theological thinking without reference to metaphysics. Their decision is equivalent to excluding any mention of an objective action of God in the sacraments, and without divine action there can be no objective presence of Christ in the sacraments.

The only coherent place for a presence of Christ in the kind of sacramentology they have chosen to do will be one that is defined exclusively in terms of the community's way of constituting itself in and through the symbolic activity that is a condition for any human self-awareness and self-identity. This certainly permits them to appeal to faith and affirm that the community can constitute itself in this way as the church of Christ only because God is at work, something that would not be admitted in the human sciences they draw on. But, however convincingly they may develop this affirmation of faith, they are never going to be able to rejoin, within the chosen terms of their systematic thinking, the simple affirmation that is being made in the Catholic reading of Christ's eucharistic words.

The value of what such theologians are saying lies in their taking seriously the human side of the sacraments or, as would be said in another context, the immanence of God without which the affirmation of his transcendence is rendered meaningless. This is an important pastoral contribution to the understanding of the sacraments. Nevertheless, pastors should remain convinced that the faith that animates their communities needs to reach out, beyond sociological aids, to the reality of God and Christ. Whatever may be the truth about the claim that modern people do not think metaphysically, and though we have suggested that probably not many people succeed in doing so even when they want to, the fact is that the Catholic liturgy takes it for granted that those who share in it believe that "this" *is* his body. Without the aid of metaphysics a Catholic theologian has nothing to add to this; he should not for that reason cast doubt on it.

Let us, then, sum up in the light of these considerations what can be said about the relations obtaining between word and sacrament. This will serve as a framework for discussing the question in terms of the other sacraments.

Stress must first be laid on the continuity that exists between word and sacrament. The word, at least in the ritual sacraments, is a permanent feature of the Christian ministry and it merges naturally with the active symbolism of the sacraments. In line with the growing awareness of the role played by language, as symbol, in the development and not simply the expression of experience, there is every reason to underline the way in which the Spirit is at work through the mediation of the network of communication established in the sacramental rites. The Christian community attaches a special significance to its use of the natural symbols of water, wine and bread. It uses them to recall and to share by faith in the saving deeds of God through the history of the chosen people. But it is also aware, as the words of the offertory in the Mass, for example, make clear, that the Christian revelation is a confirmation of the work of creation and that the salvation brought by Christ has an integrally human and cosmic significance. The symbolic activity creates a space in which response to the word by faith can become fully itself in a celebration of the word, of salvation and of the human situation that is brought under the influence of Christ.

These moments of word and of response to the word are specifically sacred moments for they involve an explicit advertence and openness to the divine initiative that makes Christian life possible. It is quite true that the salvation being brought by Christ looks beyond the distinction between sacred and profane and will finally render it superfluous, for it is a salvation of all that is created and only sin is opposed to it. But until salvation is fully achieved, as long as believers are involved in the ongoing process of bringing Christian values into the world, explicitly sacred interludes remain necessary. In them the ambiguities of the Christian task are brought into the clear light of the gospel and Christians join in common worship of the divine Trinity. The symbolism of word and active response becomes a bearer of the Spirit when it is appropriated in faith and commitment by the community gathered in the name of Christ. Its human significance, which can constantly reveal new and unsuspected dimensions to those who share in it with sensitivity, is taken up by faith and expanded. It can become a medium for communication with the self, with the community and with the creative and redemptive Trinity. Here already the receptiveness of faith alternates with the response of worship and the acceptance of mission; and all of this is the presence of Christ through the Spirit.

The question becomes reasonable: Could the Spirit give more to the community of faith? The answer is that he has already done so when the Father sent his Son into the world and thereby determined once for all that a man should be the mediator of the further gift of the Spirit. The assembly of the word, with all its richness, becomes the truly sacramental assembly when that mediator, raised up to the Father, becomes personally present within it. Raised up, he is bringing his mission to its accomplishment in those who believe. Raised up, he exercises his power of cosmic renewal and appropriates for himself the actions and the symbols charged with the community's faith and makes them the medium of his personal presence. There is no discontinuity with the word, only transcendence.

The word about Christ and the word to Christ merge into the sacramental word uttered in his name and the Word incarnate is present. The presence of the Word cannot be deduced from the other words; it is pure gift. The reception of the ministry of the word in the faith of the community blends into worship and commitment, and then, gratuitously, this is joined through the symbols with the present worship of Christ, the giver of the Spirit.

This is incorporation into the inward life of the Trinity in which the Word goes out from the Father and returns to him in a union of love forged by the Spirit. The community's worship of the Father in the Son issues from the Father himself and is sustained and strengthened by the Spirit. Here, giving becomes receiving and receiving, giving; but at the heart of all is the mystery of the Trinity, the God who gives himself to his creatures. The gift of Christ in the Eucharist sums up the mystery; baptism is the first gift because it allows access to the Eucharist.

6.4 THE LANGUAGE OF SACRAMENTAL REALISM

An Aquinas, typical in this of the leading medieval theologians, when faced with the mystery of the sacramental presence of the risen Christ, drew upon all the resources of his knowledge of God and creation in order to describe how it can come about. His knowledge of creation was born, not of an enquiry into natures and functions, as is modern science for whose forebears St. Thomas had respect, but of an unrelenting investigation into existence, *esse*, the object of authentic metaphysics. Existence was for him the single undeniable clue that God leaves everywhere in his creation, testifying to his constant presence and sustaining activity. Because he had to use some word for it, and because he made clear what he meant by the word, Aquinas named the individual reality that truly exists, whether personal or not, "substance."

History was to prove that the choice was unfortunate because the human mind, avid for concepts and images corresponding to them, seems doomed to slide away from the existential reference of the word "substance" and to take it to signify who knows what kind of shapeless mass underlying the immediately observable. Part of the task of rediscovering existence or, more precisely, existing realities, is to uproot the word from the images and concepts we are tempted to form when we read it in a medieval text and plunge back with it into the experience of what is real.

Substance, just like existence, can only be seized in its utter originality by an act of concrete, individual, existential judgment. Whatever it is that we affirm to exist, in the strong sense of that word, is, by that very fact, "substance." Were it not for the reality of the "substance"—the objectively given person or thing—our act of judgment would not be existential, would not be the affirmation of our openness to the other in all its uniqueness. Once we open ourselves to the other we can begin to express, in the concepts or ideas we form of it under its tutelage, so much as we perceive of its own richness of being. Our concepts of it may increase and grow more complex as we let ourselves be drawn into its individual mystery through familiarity with it. We may even subject the other to the more refined conceptualization of the experimental sciences. All of this, in one way or another, will reveal progressively more and more of its existential richness; but none of it will master its simple givenness in existence, its simple act of being and doing, perhaps its personhood, with its own knowing and loving, in all their inalienability.

Love for the other is much more ready than is knowledge to accept the originality of the other; but knowledge is called upon to do so too when, in its act of existential judgment, it simply acknowledges the other. When it gives way to its urge to dominate the other, knowledge even goes so far as to preempt a word like "substance" and pervert its original meaning, turning it into yet another conceptual label but this time attached to what is radically resistant to conceptualization, existence. Now the word that was meant to be a recognition of the other's true "substance" or individual reality becomes just another way of looking at the other, a way of abstracting from its existence, generalizing it and ranging it along-side other concepts. But now it has no true function, because concepts ignore existence; so "substance" becomes meaningless and dies.

If, then, the attempt is made to leave aside all but the most primitive of concepts and to concentrate on the utter purity of an existential judgment which expresses our first, uncomplicated recognition of the other as other—perhaps when we say: "Why, it is you"—then the authentic meaning of "substance" is given because it has been instinctively recognized simply in the recognition of the identity of the other. Then, perhaps, it will suddenly become startlingly obvious why, in the mouth of a St. Thomas, the word "transubstantiation," in spite of its awkwardness, needs no explanation. It is what must be said if the words, "This is my body," are to have the realist meaning attributed to them in the Catholic tradition. It would be tempting to say that the word makes no appeal to any philosophy, that it simply reflects the judgment that this is no longer bread but Christ himself, were it not for the fact that St. Thomas found the word "substance" in Aristotle and was concerned, for his own reasons, to suggest that Aristotle attached to it the same existential meaning as did St. Thomas himself.

Certainly, the Council of Trent had no such academic preoccupations and simply used the current theological vocabulary in order to say that the Catholic tradition attaches a realist signification to the words of institution of the Eucharist. Both Council and theologian were convinced that this could be verified only by an appeal to the infinite power of God, the one, adds St. Thomas, who has power over the totality of being and who can take away whatever it is that distinguishes one being from another (cf. *Summa theol.*, III, q. 75, a. 4 ad 3). Even if this last remark—which conceals a quite staggering thought—is not insisted upon, both faith and theology have still to account for the observable elements of bread and wine. Their symbolic function requires no further explanation, but in terms of existence they are claimed to be less profoundly rooted in it than is substance so that there is no reason for them to share the fate of substance. This is not the place to develop the implications of this for enough has been said to indicate that transsubstantiation has nothing to do with scholastic cosmology. Metaphysics has nothing to do with theories about the nature of matter, which are the concern of cosmology; metaphysics' only concern is existence. The fact that it can be confused with cosmology is another example of how the human mind takes flight from existence and prefers the manageable concepts that it abstracts from existing realities.

The active presence of Christ claimed for baptism led the scholastics to propose for it a scheme of concepts which may be much more difficult to explain in the climate of contemporary thought. St. Thomas, referring to a theory already put forward by an Eastern theologian, St. John Damascene (c. 650-c. 750), suggested that the neo-platonic thinking of the latter could be aligned with the Western way of thinking about divine activity if Aristotle's concept of instrumental causality were introduced. Then the more mystical view of divine energy being mediated to man through the humanity of Christ and through the sacramental rites could be formulated with greater conceptual precision by saying that the divine Trinity, the source of all created good, acts as the principal cause of whatever effects are attributed to the sacrament, and uses as its instruments, first the humanity of Christ, united to the Son, and then the elements of the liturgical symbol.

It is very easy to criticize this conceptual scheme from the point of view of Christian personalism. As well as that, when it is cut off from the whole theology it implicitly refers to, it can be incomprehensible. There is little help to be found in the more bland style of Trent's condemnation of anyone who shall say "that the sacraments of the New Law do not contain the grace which they signify, or that they do not confer that grace on those who place no obstacle in its way, as though they were only outward signs of grace" (7th Session, can. 6; NR 418). There is, first of all, the difficulty about making such a broad generalization about the sacraments. Even more serious is the objection sometimes made that, in spite of the vagueness of the word "confer," a schema of "causal" thought is being used, derived from an outmoded form of physics, which has no place in an account of the mystery of Christian salvation. This is probably the principal reason why contemporary theologians are drawn to explain the efficacy of the sacraments in terms of their symbolism. They are obviously not suggesting, in opposition to Trent, that the sacraments are only outward signs of grace. They are quite clear in their insistence that an anthropological understanding of symbol, as constitutive of man in society, attributes a real efficacy to the sacrament, one that God "takes up" into his saving initiative, and one that has the advantage of elevating the believer from the status of a recipient who places no obstacle to that of an active participant.

Now, it is quite evident that the personalistic view is the one that inspires the present inquiry, for it corresponds to one of the senses being given to "realism." At the same time, however, the complementary point is being made that Christian personalism is a gift of grace. We have seen how complex is the interplay of the divine and the human, the transcendent and the immanent, in this event of grace. To call it "cooperation" between God and man is to fall into the trap of rationalization and to end up with that synergism which the Reform, reaching back to the authentic medieval theology of grace, rejected with such good reason. The truth is to be found in that hardly expressible harmony between the Creator of all and the created person that the dialectic of the Reform, with its inflexible "either God or man," failed to grasp.

The problem for the theologian is how to express the barely expressible. The medieval solution was to take one's time over it and to explore all the facets of the event of grace, subjecting each of them to as careful an analysis as was possible. An Aquinas wrote a *Summa* with this intention, each of its sections being organically related to the whole. When he came to formulating a general theory of the sacraments, he made the choice of first developing their significance as symbolic actions of the community and then locating this whole discussion in a broader, strictly theological context centered on the saving initiative of God in Christ. This was eminently reasonable, not only because the New Testament speaks in this way about baptism and the Eucharist, but also because he had already analyzed, in terms of both God and man, the event of grace and could assume that that part of his system had already been assimilated. It will, perhaps, be conceded that his procedure is acceptable but it is likely that it will still be maintained that his judgment was poor in selecting the category of "cause" to express what he had to say about God's initiative in the sacraments.

An adequate reply to this objection, which touches post-medieval as well as medieval theology, both the Catholic and the Reformed traditions, and even certain currents in post-Reformation Eastern theology, would involve a full-scale discussion of theological method and the categories it needs to use when statements are being made about God. This is clearly not possible here; but the key to the solution adopted over so many centuries and in so widespread a spectrum of religious traditions will be found in the so-called five ways to the existence of God, proposed in their classic Christian form by St. Thomas. Their theological significance lies, not in any application they may have to the question of whether

God exists, but in the fact that they are a statement and a justification of the fundamental categories that St. Thomas considered necessary if any talk about God is to have sense in terms of human experience. Whether these categories—they are the three used in the judgments that God is the final, exemplar and efficient cause of all reality—were originally elaborated by Plato or Aristotle is of slight importance. Jewish and Islamic philosophers had already given them new significance in a religious context before, and parallel to, their use in Christian theology. St. Thomas, in any case, attached to them their full Christian significance when he modified them in such a way that they could be applied to the God who creates all things out of nothing.

In particular, the category of efficient cause was adopted by Aquinas to express the creative activity of the Blessed Trinity; he was not the first to do this but he ensured the almost universal acceptance of the proposal in the Western church. This places theologians who agree with the arguments he used to justify his choice in an embarrassing position. Or, at least, they should be embarrassed if they have grasped the fact that the effect of God's creative activity is existence, the being-real of anything that is real. Now, existence, we have been insisting, cannot be expressed in a concept; it is known only in an existential judgment when the knower is seized by the reality of the other. For much greater reason the One who creates existence out of nothing cannot be conceptualized, only affirmed as the Other from whom all others derive their existence.

How, then, can we talk about this Creator; how can we talk about his act of creation? All of this is equally resistant to concepts. Though no one, perhaps, understood this better than St. Thomas, he still persisted in proposing the concept of efficient causality as a way of speaking about God's creative action. He was acutely aware of the almost compelling necessity that, once one has discovered or rediscovered existence, and has gone on from that to look towards God, the fullness of existence, one should favor silence; and at the end of his life this is what he did. The whole tradition of negative theology, more Greek than Latin, though it was loquacious enough, really chose silence. The only way out of negative theology that has ever been discovered, the only way there is to say something positive about God and about his creative and saving activity, however imperfect the concept must be acknowledged to be, relies in the last analysis on the conviction that it is legitimate and helpful to speak of the act of creation as an exercise of efficient causality. Though the theological implications of this are immense, it does not seem very different from the quite natural affirmation of the believer that God made the world. Because this kind of thinking entered naturally into the later Jewish heritage of the New-Testament writers it permitted them to speak almost unreflectively of God's saving act and to make it the presupposition of their whole belief. The medievals, thoroughly familiar with the theological consequences of agnosticism, were obliged to clarify the presupposition, assess the limitations of their concepts and then, with full awareness of what they were doing, proceed to use the only concepts that are at the disposal of the believer to "speak" about the mystery of God. They were, in particular, perfectly conscious of the likelihood that their use of the term "efficient cause" for God would conjure up for untutored minds the shades of determinism. For this reason they analyzed at length the method to be used when applying the term to God and then took the necessary risk of using it.

Given this way of thinking about the fundamental relations that exist between man and God, there is nothing novel about the introduction of efficient causality into accounts of the saving action of God in Christ and then of both in the sacraments. It is, of course, required that those who encounter this way of speaking about the sacraments be aware of the immense effort of theological thinking that is concealed in the simple word "cause." It is used, after all has been said that can be said about the human side of sacramental practice, to place emphasis on the divine initiative of salvation in Christ which is believed to be still active in the sacramental space. It may, of course, quite feasibly be argued that this use of the word, whatever intelligibility it may hold for the initiated, cannot fail to provoke in the uninformed or the unconvinced all sorts of misleading images and ideas. Since what is at stake is a concept, a more suitable one may be sought out, so long, that is, as it is capable of expressing the existential reality of the dependence of salvation on God. If the sole difficulty about the idea of "cause" is that it assumes that God is truly active in the world, and if it is this assumption that a theologian is trying to dispense with because he wants to express transcendence in purely immanent terms, then, of course, it is pointless to look for substitutes.

But if it is agreed that God's saving presence in the sacraments transcends the inter-personal relationships set up in the community, though it does manifest itself through and in them, then categories expressing inter-personal love will best be chosen to speak of the new possibility of union with Christ that is offered. But if the mystery of divine love is not to be dissipated in pietistic sentiment, it is necessary to speak of God's intervention in Christ as one of a love that is creative. The creative love of God, it will be said, is such that it achieves salvation through the mediation of the risen Christ as he exercises his power of cosmic renewal. To appeal to the unique power of the risen Christ in his cosmic role is sufficient to mark out the newness of baptism and the Eucharist in relation to the ministry of the word.

6.5 A EUCHARISTIC HERMENEUTIC

Discussion of word and sacrament and their mutual relation has led to a wide-ranging examination of some of the most fundamental questions of theology, including the question of how to do theology. This is not surprising, for attitudes to the word-sacrament debate reveal deep-seated options that have been made concerning the possibility and extent of our knowledge of God and these inevitably color every theological statement that follows. The view has been put forward here that the only way out of the conceptual maze that contemporary theologians are constructing for themselves lies in the rediscovery of the act of existence and of its primordial significance for all forms of thought. Existence is not complicated; it is the thing that makes children laugh when they discover something new. Thinking about it is hard only because thinking must use concepts and concepts have their own kind of seductive existence which distracts from the simple givenness of true existence.

At the center of Catholic understanding of the church there is this kind of simple givenness about the eucharistic presence of Christ. From this unique example of existence, which widens the Catholic perception of what is real, it is legitimate to formulate what has already been referred to in passing, a general hermeneutic of theology. A hermeneutic is a method for interpreting a text and Christian theologians have several special hermeneutic methods for determining the meaning of Scripture, of the historic confessions of the faith and of all the other texts given in the tradition. A general hermeneutic is presupposed to all of these and textual scholars, when they have reflected on what they are doing, are ready to admit that they work with such presuppositions.

There can be more than one general hermeneutic influencing in this way even the seemingly most straightforward reading of a text. When it comes to systematic theology, general hermeneutics, presuppositions, abound, though it is often difficult, even for those who are influenced by them, to discern their structure. They are inevitably philosophical in nature, though probably influenced, so it would seem, by religious intuitions characteristic of the theologian's own community tradition. It has been made plain enough that the philosophical hermeneutic being used in these pages is the one offered by a philosophy of the act of existence which is signified by the word "is" in a true judgment about reality. However, this philosophical option, which is also a conviction, is taken up and confirmed by the statement about Christ's eucharistic presence that is made, prior to any reflection, in the Catholic community. This means that the God spoken about according to this hermeneutic is, in general terms, the creator of existence; and, in specific terms, the God who brings about the eucharistic existence of Christ. It is of this God that the Scriptures speak; this is the kind of God he is.

It could, of course, be said that this general hermeneutic is itself taken up and confirmed by the statement about the identity of Christ that is now made, prior to any reflection, in the Christian community and the complementary statement that he is living in glory. But these existential statements about Christ are, in fact, implied in the eucharistic statement. The latter has the advantage of including the others and placing them in the context of their present significance for the Christian community. It also provides the opportunity for theology to be situated within the living worship of the community, not by some sort of personal adjustment that the theologian must make in his own Christian existence, but by the very nature of his work.

CHAPTER SEVEN:
RECONCILIATION:
REALITY AND SACRAMENT

THE CATHOLIC TEACHING on the sacramental nature of reconciliation or penance provides one of the most instructive examples that can be used for clarifying the sacramental idea and for formulating the relation between word and sacrament. This is because it gives a case where the intensely personal event of individual conversion, obviously the concern of the ministry of the word, is said to be linked in some inescapable fashion with a liturgical, and therefore public, ceremony of the Christian community. It is an undisputed fact that a baptized Christian's resolve to turn away from personal involvement in unchristian behavior must be a decision that springs from a renewed affirmation of the person's deepest convictions and must be implemented through a fresh and sustained commitment to the way of the gospel. There is a clear role here for the ministry of the word to play, not only the ministry of formal preaching but, in addition, that which can be exercised in numberless ways by the whole Christian community, whether by way of example or by way of direct persuasion and encouragement. Since no one will deny that the final decision must be made by the individual concerned, the function assigned by the Catholic tradition to the sacrament seems to be very much in need of justification.

7.1 PERSONAL CONVERSION AND SACRAMENT

No doubt impressed by the personalist argument, even Catholic theologians and pastors can increasingly be found who show signs of being hesitant about the role of the sacrament. Penitential services and different forms of counselling, which are ministries of the word, more and more are taking the place of sacramental confession. If they are made sacramental by genuine conversion on the side of the participants and by absolution, whether general or individual, it may not be always clearly realized just how this differs from the rest of the service or pastoral discussion. Among theologians who are concerned to preserve a distinction there is a fairly widespread inclination to interpret the strictly sacramental phase as a ceremony of reconciliation with the church. This is doubtless a result of the emphasis laid by the Second Vatican Council on the communitary structure of the church and of an understanding that it is the whole community that is injured by the sinfulness of the individual.

It has its origins too in more widespread awareness of the extraordinarily complex history of penance in the church which reveals how many different forms public penance has taken over the centuries. Only in the sixth century did the idea begin to take hold that public penance could be repeated, though in a less formal way, during the lifetime of an individual. Only after a thousand years of the Christian era was absolution regularly pronounced immediately after confession of sin. Before that a period of rigorous penance normally intervened during which the penitent was excluded from the assembly of the Eucharist. In these circumstances the salient aspect of absolution was precisely that of reconciliation with the community and readmission to the Eucharist. If this is taken to be the meaning of absolution, its immediate efficacy is to be stated in terms of ecclesial communion; but this act of the church, which is a sacrament of salvation, is to be taken as ratified by God or, in less juridical language, as a symbol of God's forgiveness.

To state that reconciliation with the Church is the direct and formal effect of sacramental absolution is not, of course, a simple conclusion of historical research; it is a theological interpretation of the historical data and has to be discussed as such. The theory was, in fact, introduced into recent theological discussion in a very technical form. It was suggested as an interpretation of a notoriously difficult passage in the writings of St. Thomas Aquinas in which the *res et sacramentum* of the sacrament of penance (this corresponds to what, in the case of baptism, has been called the abiding sacrament) is identified with the penitent's sorrow for his sins (cf. *Summa theol.*, III, q. 84, a. 1 ad 3). The passage will be examined below; here it is sufficient to note that the difficulties connected with its interpretation led to the proposal that, instead of being equated with sorrow, the *res et sacramentum* should be said to be reconciliation with the church. This may not look like an earth-shaking suggestion but it prepared the way for a gradual erosion of the mystery-aspect of the sacrament and, for that reason, of its intensely personal nature. This requires some explanation.

First of all, some way must be found of putting in order the scattered and sometimes complex elements that are associated with the sacrament of penance: the subtleties of the religious psychology of conversion, questions concerning the nature of sin and conscience, the radical developments which public penance has known, the role of the church and the sacrament. The real event around which all of these are ranged is that of the conversion of a baptized Christian so that it is in terms of it that they should all be discussed. They need to be discussed from two points of view: existentially, or from the point of view of the person, and christologically, from the point of view of the salvation that Christ brings.

Existentially, the question of using the sacrament of penance arises only at the end of a personal experience of conversion or, at least, when the problem of extricating oneself from a situation understood as sinful becomes a matter of personal urgency. Seen as an integral part of this experience, the sacrament is to be interpreted in correspondingly personalist terms. As much goes into this personal experience as constitutes the Christian life of the individual concerned, whether it be standards that he has integrated into his own moral awareness or what he has only partially assimilated from outside, from his family and friends, from what he grasps of the moral teaching of the gospel and the church. If he is truly a Christian and not simply one seeking after ethical ideals, he will be more or less vividly aware that his project of conversion is something that he cannot achieve unaided, by his personal effort, even though he cannot achieve it without that effort. He will be more or less conscious of a deep-seated personal conviction that the meaning of Christ, to whom he belongs by baptism, is being shown to him in his present situation, that his desire for self-reform is already the work of Christ who, in that hidden way, is bringing the mercy and forgiveness of God.

The sacrament of penance itself, when it is fitted into this existential perspective, may not appear to differ in any important way from what has preceded it, though it may be experienced as a disagreeable obligation imposed by the church. Then, as soon as church obligations are no longer taken for granted, the question begins to be asked whether or not there is any intrinsic justification for the sacrament since, if the process of conversion is a genuine one, the principal purpose of the sacrament has already been attained. Once the question has been posed in such terms it almost answers itself so that the search begins for other positive values that can reasonably be attached to the sacramental celebration.

Sometimes justification will be sought in the uncertain hypotheses of psychotherapy. A more appropriate understanding of the priestly ministry will suggest advantages more closely linked with the message of the gospel and the counselling of the individual's conscience that it requires. The need to relate conversion to the preaching of the word will bring penitential services to the fore and emphasis will be laid on the communal character of sin and salvation. Given the question that has been posed, the theory of reconciliation with the church as a prelude to joining again in the celebration of the Eucharist begins to look like an ideal solution and one, moreover, that avoids narrow individualism. Now, many of these values are, in fact, to be found or could be found in the liturgical ceremony of penance, and one or more of them might well be stressed in particular circumstances. The difficulty is that, with the possible exception of reconciliation with the church, all the authentic values being suggested belong to the ministry of the word; to detail them contributes little that helps in solving the problem of why penance is held to be a sacrament in the strict sense.

It remains to be seen whether the christological approach to conversion will be more enlightening. Not coincidentally, it is this approach that originally permitted penance to be classified as a sacrament. Theological reflection on the church's ministry of reconciliation did not succeed for many centuries in coming to anything like a consensus as to what it is that gives distinctiveness to the central ceremonies of confession and absolution. The various forms that these exterior signs of conversion and reconciliation took bear witness to the changing methods of pastoral care and to the different ways in which they were perceived by the faithful through the centuries and into the medieval church. In the important twelfth-century effort to organize sacramental teaching penance offered an intractable problem. In a way that would be astonishing for post-Tridentine theology, the medievals easily took it for granted that a Christian who presented himself for absolution was already converted from sin and that he was already decided to repair whatever injury he had done to others. This assumption had nothing to do with public penance already performed for that was no longer common; it derived rather from their understanding of conversion itself.

In spite of this, their explanation of the liturgical ceremony that was later received by the church was not formulated in terms of reconciliation to the church and readmission to the Eucharist, even though this would have been in harmony with the much more frequent use of excommunication at that time. Their account of the sacrament was based instead on their understanding of sin as an offense against God and on their faith in the Incarnation. They were well aware of the consequences for society of sin and, within the limits of the society they knew, they prescribed the remedies that had to be taken. But their faith in creation and salvation convinced them that offense against man is offense against God and that Christ had come to restore the social order by means of a more fundamental restoration of man's relations with God.

In this context they developed a christological explanation of the strict sacramentality of penance, one which takes up the existential account of conversion and reinterprets it in the light of the Incarnation. The center of gravity shifts away from the experience of conversion as a personal undertaking to the total gratuitousness of the mercy and forgiveness of God as revealed in Christ.

The pastoral intention of the move in emphasis is to draw attention beyond the struggle of the individual conscience and into the mystery of divine creative love. As has now been stressed several times, the creative forgiveness of God is creative because, unlike human forgiveness which at best can encourage a change of heart in the one who is forgiven, the divine forgiveness makes itself known in that very change of the sinner's heart.

What the repentant sinner experiences as his own deeply personal struggle culminating in hard-won decision is, as on later reflection he may well come to recognize, the power of God's forgiving love. Even though the repentant sinner may quite naturally experience the negative side of being forgiven his offenses, he has in fact not simply turned his back on sin; he has given himself once more to God, for God's love for him creates in him the response of love. In addition, the Incarnation of the Word has as its consequence that this sending of the Spirit of love does not occur apart from Christ, that, indeed, he is actively engaged in the conversion of the sinner. Now, the sacramental idea expresses the belief that this saving intervention of Christ continues even after the resurrection and ascension and that it maintains its incarnational realism through the sacramental action.

What the medieval theologians did, and the question has not been seriously taken up in any other way since they did it, was to propose that this mystery of Christian grace is represented symbolically in the central rite of the ministry of reconciliation. They added that the minister's role is exercised in virtue of the "power of the keys," this being a symbolic (and not a juridical) allusion to *Matthew*, 16:19, which was specified by reference to *Matthew*, 18:18, *Luke*, 24:47 and, in particular, *John*, 20:21-23, in which the risen Christ is seen giving his disciples the Holy Spirit to forgive sins. At first sight this may well seem to be a piece of deductive theology on the part of the medievals, which simply transfers to the special case of penance a theory which has been worked out to fit the case of infant baptism. The objection has often been made that the theory just does not suit penance and does not even take account of the medievals' own supposition that conversion has normally taken place before the sacrament is celebrated. The difficulty is a valid one; thinking about it may help to clarify some of the problems connected with the question of word and sacrament.

7.2 THE CLASSICAL THEORY OF THE SACRAMENT

There is no reason to doubt that when the theologians of the twelfth and thirteenth centuries undertook a systematic discussion of penance, and of marriage as well, they had already devised a theoretical scheme of concepts which fitted the major sacraments, baptism and the Eucharist, and which they assumed would be verified also in the case of these others. The scheme, developed from Augustine's theology of baptism, comprised the three notions of visible symbol (*sacramentum tantum*), the gift of the sanctifying Spirit (*res*) and the abiding sacrament (*res et sacramentum*). This last category had proved its worth in the development of the theology of the baptismal character and of the eucharistic presence. The attempt would therefore be made to see whether it might not be equally illuminating in the case of penance.

As to the gift of the Spirit conveyed by the sacrament of penance, the *res*, this was universally identified as the remission or forgiveness of sin committed after baptism. There was, however, disagreement as to what constitutes the visible symbol, the *sacramentum tantum*. What might be called the "clerical" party, though its adherents used a christological argument, suggested that it should be seen in the priestly minister who pronounces the words of absolution. In him, they claimed, is to be found the full symbolization of the Christ who forgives, and it is through this ministry that he actually forgives the sinner. St. Thomas, on the contrary, showed himself much more conscious of the permanent sacramental significance of baptism and the character it gives, and of the need to integrate the activity of the repentant sinner into the structure of the sacramental symbol. He proposed that the visible symbol should be seen as a joint action of penitent and minister, the interaction of the two forming the existential symbol of Christ actually imparting his forgiveness to one who shows himself ready to receive it. In detail, St. Thomas saw the sacramental symbol as made up of the penitent's outward expression of sorrow, together with his confession of sinfulness and his manifest readiness to make amends, and of the minister's words of absolution. This common symbolic action brings about, through the intervention of Christ, the remission of sin.

Apart from giving this further example of what is to be understood when the baptismal character is said to be a capacity for sacramental worship, St. Thomas was concerned to integrate sacramental practice with his moral theology. The mystery of grace, in which God's initiative becomes effective in the response of the human person, should, he was convinced, be reflected in the sacramental rite. This left the third member of the conceptual scheme to be accounted for, the *res et sacramentum*, the abiding sacrament. Modern readers should not lose patience too quickly with the apparent artificiality of this medieval concern for precision; it was prompted by a conviction that the sacraments are more than passing ceremonies, that they should be seen as imparting a lasting quality determining the future life-style of those who share in them. The discussion on the nature of the *res et sacramentum* is really concerned with this.

The point being made in the term, *res et sacramentum*, had been illustrated in its being applied to the baptismal character, to the character of orders and to the real presence of Christ in the Eucharist. Though all of these were accepted as gifts or effects of the sacraments, and therefore as *res* or "realities signified and given," they were seen to be, not in themselves the gift of the Spirit sanctifying the individual, but rather structural elements in that living sacrament of the Trinity and of the mediation of Christ which is the church, and so as *sacramentum*, sacrament as well as *res*.

If, then, one generalizes this complex concept, one will take it that it always includes some reference to the visible structure of the earthly church as this is sacramental or expressive of the mystery of salvation. This is why those modern theologians who have grasped what the medievals were getting at are attracted by the proposal that the *res et sacramentum* of penance should be identified as reconciliation with the church of the Eucharist, for here is something that evidently belongs to the sacrament of the church. The curious thing is that St. Thomas, who was alert to the ecclesial implications of the sacraments, chose a more difficult solution. He preferred to say that the *res et sacramentum* of penance is the penitent's sorrow for sin and of such a kind as is based on faith in the saving power of Christ's mysteries and already inspired by the gift of the Spirit, the repentant sinner's renewed love for God.

There are very weighty difficulties attached to this solution and we shall have to return to them; but for the moment let us leave them aside and simply consider the understanding of the nature of the church revealed in the proposed solution, it being remembered that the *res et sacramentum* is assumed to be ecclesial in some way. Notable, first of all, is the readiness to open up for the term *res et sacramentum* a new field of signification. In the case of baptism the term signifies an abiding incorporation into the church and into the risen Christ which, though directed towards full incorporation, is not of itself the sanctifying gift of the Spirit. When it comes to penance, however, the same term is used to signify sorrow for sin which has certainly been expressed in the church's ritual but is at the same time a sorrow which implies personal acceptance of the sanctifying Spirit. This indicates an awareness of the fact that the term "sacrament" is an analogous one, that is to say, a single term which is applied to several cases, having certain common characteristics but, for all that, differing very considerably among themselves. This has already been demonstrated by the fact that both the real presence of the Eucharist and the character of baptism, though they obviously differ widely one from the other, can both be called an "abiding sacrament." With the application of the same term to sorrow for sin, expressed in the rite of penance, the idea of abiding sacrament is seen to be capable of taking up a reality belonging to the moral order, to the actual state of heart of the penitent.

This now indicates a second noteworthy point, one which has to do with the concept of the church that is implied when the personal, moral attitude of a baptized Christian is seen as ecclesial, pertaining to the church as sacrament. Now a new depth is discovered in the idea of "reconciliation with the church." This is no longer a simple celebration of readmission to the Eucharist made by an authorized minister of the community and "ratified" by God, which is what most present-day authors seem to be suggesting. Restoration of communion is certainly granted but this reconciliation with the church is made real because the individual penitent who takes part in the reconciliation ceremony is genuinely reunited with the church in charity. The reconciliation is at once "sacramental" and "mental," in the terms of St. Augustine's ecclesiology. The sacrament of penance is thus seen as a typical event in the life of the church as a sacrament of the Trinity, for the symbol enacted by penitent and minister, which calls upon the mediation of Christ, is made real by the presence of Christ in the minister and by the movement, awakened in the penitent by the Spirit, away from sin and towards the Father. Christ's sacramental mediation is brought to its achievement in the ecclesial sign of life in the Trinity. There are, it has been said, difficulties about this account of the sacrament of penance and it is likely that they will spontaneously formulate themselves at first in a vague uneasiness about the way that contrition has apparently been introduced into the sacramental rite itself, whereas it is well known that, according to traditional Catholic teaching, the sacrament brings the forgiveness of sin. If true contrition is required for the sacrament itself, this seems to be equivalent to saying that the sacrament is no longer necessary, for true contrition is inspired by love of God and, once that gift has been received from the Spirit, sin is already forgiven. It seems best to address this difficulty and all the others that spring from it by analyzing the text of St. Thomas that lies at the source of the confusion. This is the same text that originally prompted modern theologians to cut through the whole discussion by making the sacrament a solemn readmission to the Eucharist without any direct efficacy in the remission of sin. The analysis of the text is, of necessity, concentrated on details. It is undertaken in the belief that the outcome is illuminating for the whole idea of sacrament.

The text is *Summa theologiae*, III, q. 84, a. 1 ad 3. Having identified the elements of the three-fold structure of the sacrament of penance (see above), St. Thomas goes on to state how they are related among themselves. Following the generally agreed principles formulated in terms of the efficacy attributed to the sacramental symbols, he says, with no further explanation:

> "The first element, taken as a whole [the *sacramentum tantum*, the ceremony performed in common by the

penitent and the absolving minister] is the cause of
the second element [the *res et sacramentum*, the interior
contrition of the penitent]; and then the first and the
second are, in their own way [*quodammodo*; in the
Piana edition], the cause of the third element [the
res, the remission of sins]."

The progression of thought is clear but it is not easy to
follow. (1) The visible sacrament is said to cause contrition, evidently by the power of Christ in the absolution.
But how can this be, seeing that an integral part of the
visible sacrament is the penitent's expression of that
same contrition now said to be caused by the visible
sacrament? Contrition seems to be presupposed to itself,
if not to cause itself. (2) Then, the visible sacrament,
in conjunction with the interior contrition, is said to
cause the remission of sin. But how can this be, since
true contrition (and it is of this that St. Thomas is
speaking) is inspired by charity, and this is possible only
if sin has already been forgiven by the creative love of
God? Forgiveness of sin seems to be presupposed to itself
and indeed, "in its own way," the cause of itself.—All of
this seems hopelessly confused; it has certainly confused
generations of readers. One might wonder whether, if
this was the best Aquinas could do, the attempt to explain
the sacrament has not foundered on its own artifice. After
all, the essential message of the gospel, Christ's an-
nouncement of forgiveness, is totally arresting because
of its simplicity.

The only answer to this is itself simple: there is more
to Christian theology than the repetition of Christ's
words. There is something missing in this theology—
whether biblical, historical or systematic—when a firm
witness of the tradition is ignored. In the case of the
systematic theology of penance, Catholic belief has not
been adequately thought through if the sacramental
reference of the forgiveness of sin is not integrated into

the presentation. The sacramentality must be seen as belonging to the essence of the forgiveness of sin, in a way that is analogous to the Eucharist's belonging to the giving of the Spirit in the church on earth. This is what St. Thomas is trying to take into account in the obscure text we are considering. This suggests that a fresh approach should be made from the side of Christian personalism, working from there towards the sacrament; it may be that this will throw fresh light on the text.

7.3 THE REALITY AND THE SACRAMENT

It might, in fact, have been more fair to Aquinas had we turned our attention first to the way in which he deals with the anti-sacramentalist position. This he summarizes as follows: "God can forgive sin without the intervention of the sacrament of penance; but he cannot do so without the sinner being repentant. It is in this way that sin is forgiven where the sacrament is unknown. Since repentance is the only indispensable requirement, it should be acknowledged as the reason why sin is remitted" (*Summa theol.*, III, q. 86, a. 6, "sed contra"). The reply (I translate freely):

> An act of true contrition is indispensable for the forgiveness of sin only because it is itself a gift inseparably joined to the gift of grace. It is this divine grace that is the ultimate source of all forgiveness of sin. And it is this grace that is active in all the sacraments. All that can be concluded from the [anti-sacramentalist] argument is that it is divine grace, much more radically than the sinner's repentance, that is responsible for the remission of sin.

In any case, adds St. Thomas, any kind of organized religion will have some form of ritual celebrating the forgiveness of sin by God. The whole weakness of the anti-sacramentalist position, so runs this reply, lies in the fact that it does not recognize, or does not sufficiently advert to, the fact that sorrow for sin is itself a gift. Deeply personal though it is, and however psychologically complex it may be, sorrow for sin is acknowledged by faith to be the emerging into human consciousness of the hidden grace of God. It betrays a fundamental misconception of the true state of affairs when a contrast is set up between personal sorrow and the sacramental offer of forgiveness.

Personal sorrow is always indispensable; but so too is divine grace; all the sacrament does is to bring into prominence the gift of God which might otherwise be overlooked. Once again we are confronted with the seeming paradox of grace: in terms of personal decision, sorrow is the condition for the remission of sin; at the same time sorrow is given by God as the experiential accompaniment of his gratuitous remission of sin. The paradox is only apparent because the first statement refers to the psychology of conversion while the second is a statement of faith made with an awareness of the absolute priority of divine grace.

It is becoming clear that the reference of the moral event of conversion to the sacrament is very far from being the arbitrary formalism that it can at first sight appear to be. It is fundamentally a recognition of the fact that the initiative in salvation lies with God. This is made more precise by faith which refers the event in the individual's life to the saving influence of Christ. Finally, there is the affirmation that this mystery of Christ is linked in a special way with the sacrament. In this last step recurs, as always, the theme of the divine logic of the Incarnation, a logic that is based on the unitive force of love, which decrees that the union with mankind initiated when the Word was made flesh is not suspended after the ascension but maintained by way of those inter-personal encounters typical of sacramental events. The difficulty about this that we are finding in the case of penance, and that is responsible for the complexity of St. Thomas's text, is a reflection of the subtle interplay of the divine initiative and human responsibility characteristic of the reconciliation of an adult Christian.

The first step towards resolving the difficulty simply requires that we envisage a way of translating into active symbols the hidden event of grace and conversion. For, though the ministry of the word is already at the service of the message of mercy, and though sharing in a penitential service is already an expression of the community's prayer for forgiveness, of the individual's sorrow and of Christ's word of absolution, there is clearly a place for a more active and more personal form of participation on the part of the individual. The various historical forms of individual penance, after all has been said that needs to be said about shifting emphases in practice and theory, are to be interpreted finally by reference to this symbolic submission of the individual, with his personal consciousness of guilt, to the offer of grace in Christ.

Given the personal nature of the individual's participation and the sincerity it obviously requires, the symbolic act on the penitent's side is not distinguishable from the reality of his situation; it is, indeed, in the act of verbalizing his situation that he comes to grips with its reality. The opportunity is clearly created by the penitent for the minister to give what Christian aid and counsel he can, first of all as one who is the penitent's like in sinfulness and faith, but also as one who holds a mission deriving from the pastoral office of the church and speaks, not in his own name, but in the name of the Spirit who guides the church.

The second step, required for grasping the sacramental idea and for going beyond the ministry of the word, is taken when it is acknowledged that, beyond the individuality of the minister and all that he can offer by way of teaching and counsel, there is a presence of the risen

Christ who has promised—and it is one of the clearest promises he made—that absolution from sin pronounced by his minister will be the bearer of the Spirit who forgives when he changes the heart of the sinner.

It is this presence of Christ, believed to be given in the sacrament, that must now be made the focus of all that has been said concerning the event of grace in conversion. This prepares the way for seizing the perhaps startling intuition that animates authentic sacramental thinking of the Catholic tradition. According to this intuition of faith, which is perfectly conscious of the fact that conversion occurs without the use of the sacrament, any conversion in the present economy of salvation carries within it a dynamism bearing it towards sacramental encounter with Christ and towards the creative love of God that is borne by the sacrament. Before such a view be rejected out of hand as preposterously unrealistic, thought should be given to the fact that a parallel claim has to be made by any Christian in respect of a universal dynamism towards Christ carried within those who are touched by the Spirit, at least if the claim is taken seriously that Christ is the unique mediator of salvation and that he saves even those who do not recognize him.

The sacramental vision, evidently, goes further and gives full weight to the words of a St. Leo the Great: "Our Redeemer's presence has passed into the sacraments" (Serm. 2, *On the Ascension*), for this is what sacramentalism means when its christological presuppositions are made explicit. The dynamism we are speaking of, borne within true conversion, is not the juridical obligation of confession imposed by the Roman church on its members. That law is secondary; its justification lies in the tenet of faith that holds that the risen Christ is to be encountered in the fulness of the way that he has chosen only when faith finds him in the sacrament. The emphasis, it should not be forgotten, is on the divine grace that makes conversion possible wherever it occurs. It is this grace that must be acknowledged, and it is adequately acknowledged only when the sinner who has been healed returns to Christ to give thanks and seeks the help of the community in preserving the grace. It should now be possible to offer a reading of the intractable text of St. Thomas around which our discussion is moving. Given the sacramental intuition, which St. Thomas clearly shared, one can construct an ideal model of what the sacrament of penance, as distinct from the ministry of the word of reconciliation, means. The model will incorporate all the elements that belong to the sacramental event when it is a sinner who takes part in it and when the hypothesis is made that he receives from Christ the forgiveness of his sin at the moment of absolution in the ceremony. That the model is perhaps seldom realized in all its details is of no importance. As an integrally ecclesial model it will serve as a criterion by which to evaluate the ecclesial significance of an event of conversion, wherever and however it occurs. It is, in fact, just such a model that results when one applies to penance the three-fold scheme, visible sacrament, abiding sacrament and moral reality.

The visible sacrament offers no difficulty; it is the action common to the penitent and the minister. It is quite normal also to identify the moral reality as the forgiveness of sin. Where we found reason for hesitation was in the suggestion that the abiding sacrament is the penitent's contrition and in the sets of relations established among the three elements of the model. Now, it is agreed that the event of grace includes both the divine initiative in Christ and the resulting personal rejection of sin by the penitent and his restored union with God and with the eucharistic community. The visible sacrament both symbolizes this complex divino-human event and, in its ideal form, brings it about. It does so by focussing its symbolism on the response that the sinner makes to Christ's offer of forgiveness and on the mercy of God expressed in the words of absolution spoken by the minister of Christ.

In the hypothesis of the ideal model, the penitent's share in the ritual, while necessarily sincere, is at first, from the psychological point of view, imperfect, for the ritual can express only his imperfect sorrow. True sorrow is attributed to the efficacy of the whole sacrament. But from the beginning the symbolism of word and action calls for that perfect sorrow which is the gift of the Spirit. When Christ's word of forgiveness is pronounced in the absolution this logic of the symbolism is fulfilled and the penitent corresponds fully to it.

When the emphasis moves from symbolism to the act of divine forgiveness and its efficacy, the structure of the symbol is respected. Stress is still laid on the active cooperation of the repentant sinner with divine grace. As a consequence, the first gift of penance is said to be the personal sorrow of the penitent and it is this that is considered to be the abiding mark left by the sacrament. Though the efficacy is here attributed to the words of absolution through which Christ is actively present, the implications of the penitent's share in the ritual are met by focussing the efficacy on his active cooperation with grace. If, in the hypothesis being made, his approach to the sacrament was inspired only by imperfect sorrow, his share in the ritual is not animated by true sorrow, the gift of Christ. It is then that the full moral efficacy of the sacrament becomes clear. The power of Christ, made present in the symbol and active in the sorrow of the penitent, brings about the remission of sin. It is, to be sure, only a relative priority that may be attributed to the penitent's sorrow with respect to the forgiveness of sin; this is why it is said to cause the remission of sin, in conjunction with the visible sacrament, "in its own way." It is nevertheless, a genuine priority from the point of view of Christian personalism and it is just this aspect of conversion that is being stressed in penance.

This, then, is the ideal model of the sacrament as understood in the light of the gospel's call to repentance and of the mission given by Christ to Peter and those

associated with him. It is ideal because it is an account
of that form of reconciliation in the time of the church
which fulfils integrally all the implications of the Incarnation. Its integral sacramentality takes into account
the sacraments already received by the penitent, not only
the abiding sacrament of baptism that makes him an
ecclesial member of the risen Christ, but also those giving
him particular status in the church, confirmation,
marriage, orders, anointing of the sick; for each of these
imparts its own dynamism towards sacramental reconciliation after serious sin. As well, penance looks forward
to participation in the Eucharist where the full implications of forgiveness are celebrated in the community.
The abiding sacrament of penance, which in this case is
identified with the personal sorrow of the absolved
sinner, accords no new status in the church but it remains
an inseparable component of the moral psychology of
the member of Christ and imposes its own obligations.

Because it is ideal, the model may not always be realized
existentially in its integrity; or, and this would be more
normal for the Catholic believer, all its parts may not be
actualized at one time. Doubtless, similar statements
would have to be made about baptism and the Eucharist
in the light of *John*, 3:5; 6:53 and *1 Tim* 2:4, in view, that
is, of the universal salvific will of God and of the necessity
for salvation of baptism and the Eucharist. The point
has, however, special relevance in the case of sacramental
penance. Quite apart from any speculation as to the
penitential practices of the church in earlier centuries,
it is important to recognize the power of the ministry of
the word in communicating the message of forgiveness
and to take account of the promptings of the Spirit
making themselves felt inwardly.

Indeed, unless we wish to lapse into a juridical form
of sacramentalism, not entirely immune from superstiti-
tion, the stress that we must place on the personal commitment of the penitent will lead us to suppose that sin
has been forgiven, in the normal course of Christian life,

before absolution is sought. Further, though counsel or instruction are frequently given on the occasion of the sacrament, they belong to a phase of the community's mission that is preparatory to the sacrament and are not reserved to the minister of penance. As well as this, the implications of sincere sorrow extend well beyond the sacramental rite and beyond the Eucharist which fulfils it into the whole life of the penitent.

In the light of this existential dispersion of the sacrament, with some of its most important elements being realized apart from the actual celebration of the rite, it becomes necessary, so it would appear, to adopt a certain flexibility about the way we understand the special presence of the risen Christ in the sacramental rite itself. It we were to envision only the ideal model of penance, then we should affirm that Christ is present in his minister in order to send the Spirit of forgiveness; and it would appear that the Scholastics, and certainly their modern successors, were thinking in this way. It would be quite useless to speculate about the "efficacy" of the sacrament in individual situations. What the Catholic spirit is seeking in the sacrament is that union with the living Christ which is believed to come about at the heart of the ministry of the word and in continuity with it; at the heart too of that whole Christian undertaking that is implicit in sorrow. It is this conviction about Christ that should animate whatever other pastoral approaches to the sacrament may be adopted. Much that has been said and written about penance since the Second Vatican Council has really been developing dimensions of the ministry of the word. This merges with the ministry of the sacrament but should not be confused with it nor allowed to replace it.

CHAPTER EIGHT:
A GENERAL THEORY OF THE
SACRAMENTAL SYSTEM

THE QUESTION of word and sacrament, it is clear, is not to be resolved in terms of any kind of opposition between the two ministries, even though an historical conflict has arisen between theories of the church that emphasize either one or the other. It has to be acknowledged that these ecclesiologies reveal deep-seated differences of perspective in the ways in which the Catholic and Protestant theological traditions perceive not only God's activity in the world but even reality itself. This has a great deal to do with the philosophical climates in which the classical theologies of each tradition were formulated; but the divergent sacramental practices of each have themselves served to maintain and foster the differences. In these circumstances, it will at least be of service to clarity if a general thesis is proposed concerning the characteristics of the sacramental order. It will be seen that, under certain aspects, it is barely distinguishable from the ministry of the word and that its distinctiveness, while not deducible from the word, is in harmony with it and with the faith that is a response to the word.

The cases of the Eucharist, baptism and penance permit the statement to be made, at least by way of a preliminary hypothesis, that word becomes sacrament in the strict sense when the risen Christ intervenes personally in the symbolic activity of the community. It is not by chance that this is confirmed to the fullest extent in the Eucharist. At the same time, the flexibility of the notion of Christ's personal intervention is illustrated by the different forms of presence attributed to him in the other two sacraments. In the case of baptism he is said to be present in a way that he is present nowhere else because in it he gives sacramental incorporation into his body, the church. In the case of penance, where the personal reconversion of the Christian is at the center, no such absolute statement about the presence of Christ can be made since, in fact, the Spirit may be given for true sorrow in many circumstances. Nevertheless, if or when the "ideal model" of penance is realized, a true presence of Christ is implicit in the efficacy attributed to the sacrament.

The special case of penance does, however, confirm what the Eucharist and baptism already indicate. In both of these it is the abiding sacrament, the *res et sacramentum*, that requires the personal presence or activity of the risen Christ. His sacramental presence constitutes the abiding sacrament of the Eucharist. In baptism the act by which he sacramentally incorporates the believer into his body gives the baptismal character. It is likewise the abiding sacrament of penance, true sorrow for sin, that draws the repentant sinner to the fulness of the sacrament so that he may submit himself to the absolution of Christ and discover the means to persevere in his resolution. Penance preserves its emphasis on the personal decision and commitment of the individual; this means that the encounter with Christ in the sacrament can be fully described in ethical terms. Nevertheless, the focus of the sacrament is on the penitent's sorrow understood as a totally gratuitous gift of the risen Christ.

The qualifications that have to be made in the case of penance suggest that the preliminary hypothesis, placing the distinctive characteristic of a sacrament in the active intervention of Christ, be itself modified. Nothing, in fact, is changed in the case of the Eucharist and baptism if attention is fixed instead on the abiding sacrament, and this facilitates the grouping together with them of penance. According to the new form of the hypothesis, the presence or activity of the risen Christ is to be related, first of all, to the abiding sacrament, however the latter is to be defined in each particular case; and the nature of Christ's activity will be said to be determined by the nature or quality of the abiding sacrament. It will be in these terms, then, that whatever is distinctive about sacraments will be defined and that the degree to which any one of the seven recognized sacraments corresponds to this criterion will be determined. The offer of sanctifying grace made by Christ in the sacraments may then be considered as a second moment or possibility. This will allow full scope for a personalist understanding of this offer of grace, while preserving the unique characteristics of the sacraments. Since the particular shape and purpose of each sacrament needs to be taken into account before the hypothesis can be confirmed, a brief survey of the other four according to the terms of the hypothesis is required.

8.1 THE ABIDING SACRAMENT: OTHER CASES

8.1.1 Marriage

It has already been said (cf. 2.2) that the sacramentality of marriage is to be sought, less in the liturgical ceremony and the exchange of vows that initiate it, than in the common life of the partners. Sacrament merges with reality here to such an extent that it is as much a human project as it is a place of grace. It would be fanciful to postulate for it anything like the special active presence of Christ in baptism. Christ can and does, of course, live in the Christian spouses and their unique relationship as persons; but there is no reason to say this presence differs in any essential way from his presence in all believers and in all who have received the Spirit. It has already been proposed that the healing of marital relations by Christ is intrinsically sacramental because the fluctuating fortunes and misfortunes of marriage, when they are situated in a context of personal and permanent fidelity, constitute the most human form that can be given to the restoration of creation by Christ. It is, precisely, not a total restoration from the beginning of married life, but a progressive attempt to let the healing power of Christ come to reality at the very sources of human life.

It is the effort to be human and Christian in this primary life-form that gives some kind of awareness of what is meant by God's fidelity to his people and by Christ's love for his church. At each level there is an alliance that is maintained for the sake of another, even in spite of failings. The kind of sacramentality that is given when those who are incorporated into Christ by baptism enter into marriage does not call for a special presence of Christ other than that given by the Spirit. It goes, of course, without saying that this kind of sacramentality has need of the Eucharist if it is to reach its fulness. It is the Eucharist that brings the sacramental presence of Christ into the lives of husband and wife; and, conversely, the spiritual sacrifice that they offer in the eucharistic sacrifice is their Christian life together.

Since it is being argued that the sacrament of marriage is itself an enduring one, it might appear logical to say that there is no need to look further for any other form of abiding sacrament. If, on the contrary, the sacrament of marriage is understood, as it sometimes is, on strict analogy with the ritual sacraments, to be confined to the ceremony of mutual consent, there seems to be a much stronger case for suggesting that a sacramental "bond" is set up between the two persons.

Theologians who adopt this position appear to think of the bond as something similar to the character of baptism; and it might presumably be said that, like the latter, it is impressed by Christ. Although this view of the sacrament is not adopted here, there is a certain symbolic truth in it; that is, it says something true about marriage and might well inculcate a proper attitude towards it, but it does so in terms that can hardly be taken literally. The restriction of sacramentality to the ceremony of consent already reveals that the fully personal character of this sacrament is not being sufficiently considered; and the same deficiency may be discovered in the notion of an objective and impersonal bond of matrimony.

The reason for talking about such a bond at all is plain to see: it is meant to safeguard the permanence and indissolubility of the marriage, and it seems to some that it is better to do this by means of a reality independent of the perhaps changeable feelings of the spouses. Now, it is in fact necessary to postulate an abiding sacrament in marriage, distinct, at least conceptually, from the sacrament, the marriage itself. The analogy that serves best, however, for understanding it is, not the character of baptism, but the abiding sacrament of penance, for the latter is thoroughly personal as the bond of marriage must be. What binds husband and wife together is quite simply the promises that they have exchanged. Once made, if they are seriously made, the promises constitute a mutual personal commitment that is independent of subsequent changes in subjective feelings about it.

Theoretically, at least, this permanence could be deduced from the kind of total commitment of oneself to another that the marital association between man and woman, and only it, requires. For Christians, faith supplies for the uncertainties attendant upon reasoning about the human situation when a conclusion, that otherwise might impose itself, is one that makes existential demands and may for that reason be resisted.

Faith understands the permanence of marriage promises in the light of Christ's reaffirmation of the creational values of marriage. It is because the values are given with creation that it is, in principle, possible to discover them without the aid of revelation. The permanent bond of fidelity is, in other words, something inhering in the marital consent itself when it is made with the seriousness and self-dedication it requires.

The liturgical ceremony developed by the church adds nothing to the intrinsic sacredness of the promises exchanged. At most, it is a recognition of the community's involvement in promises which, however private they may seem, concern the whole fabric of the church as the sacrament of salvation. For this reason the ceremony makes explicit the implications of the promises as they are understood in Christian faith and as they correspond to authentic humanity.

What is being said here about the marriage bond is, evidently, a matter of theological opinion, being based on the personal nature of marriage as a human reality which becomes sacramental when both partners are incorporated sacramentally into Christ and accept, by faith, Christ's reaffirmation of the intrinsic values of the promises. The jurisprudence of the Catholic church in marital cases, while it shows concern for the personal factors involved, is necessarily based on a more abstract, juridical concept of marriage. There is a presumption made in law that two baptized people who enter into marriage, in a form approved by the church, incorporate into their "contract" the teaching of Christ; anything to the contrary requires proof. The question of personal faith as such is not raised in law and it is hard to see how it could be; the fact of baptism is taken as juridically verifiable and sufficient to create the presumption. A theology of marriage, on the contrary, cannot ignore the part played in the sacrament by the faith of the persons

involved, even though, as it seems, a humanistic understanding of the implications of marriage could result in
a bond just as stable as that of Christian marriage.

If faith is lacking in even one of the partners to a
Christian marriage it is hard to see how a sacrament is
given, for the purely sacramental incorporation into
Christ and the church given by the baptismal character
is inactive without faith. The fact also that one of the
partners is not baptized prevents their union from being
incorporated into the life of the church in the way that is
required for full sacramentality. There is, however, no
reason to deny that Christ's restoration of creation is
taking place in all authentic marriages, whether they are
sacramental in the full sense or not; just the contrary
must be believed to be true. The sacrament, as is the
case with baptism, the Eucharist or penance, comes into
being where Christ's universal mediation is explicitly
recognized and celebrated. The mystery of salvation
extends to all human beings and is at work in all.

Another juridical abstraction is revealed in legal
terminology when the term "institution" is used with
reference to the objective structure of marriage, held to be
adhered to by the contracting parties. Once again, this is
adequate for juridical reasoning, even though the term
seems to an outsider to betray a positivistic concept of
law. It remains a matter of considerable interest that
church law recognizes the "contract" as fully entered into
only when the marriage has been consummated; here,
account is being taken of the integrally human implications of the marriage promises. A theology of marriage
needs to attach a similar personal understanding to the
concept of "institution." It is not to be thought of as
in some fashion extrinsic to the marital promises themselves; it is, in fact, the "bond" or abiding sacrament
formed by the husband and wife when they vow themselves to each other in the way that Christ has revealed
as being in harmony with the Creator's design.

If, now, it is asked whether Christ intervenes personally to give the abiding sacrament of marriage, the answer will have to be negative. His intervention in the sacrament of baptism and his presence in the faith of the partners are enough; and, as has been said, Christ comes constantly in the Eucharist to those who are married. From this point of view, and if marriage is considered in isolation from the integral sacramental system, it will be seen as placed at the limits, or even outside, the strictly sacramental sphere. On the contrary, when it is considered as a way of life entered upon by two baptized members of Christ, and one which represents Christ's saving power active at the very sources of human life, its love and abiding fidelity will be seen as one of the most striking manifestations of the life of the church as sacrament of the Blessed Trinity. Without this, the church would not be a sacrament and the sacraments would be empty rituals. If the fidelity were an impossible task for humans, Christ's salvation would not reach into the deepest recesses of human personality. When so much is at stake, marriage, just because it is human, stands at the heart of the meaning of all the sacraments where reality itself can become a sacrament.

8.1.2 Orders

The strictly sacramental nature of the ordained ministry emerges directly and unequivocally from the doctrine of the Eucharist and from the clear distinction that is there given between the ministry of the word and the ministry of the sacraments. It is quite true that the Second Vatican Council in its descriptions of the sacrament of orders was concerned to overcome any apparent opposition between the two forms of ministry. It was able to do this because it made its point of departure an account of the college of bishops where the particular forms of ministry are taken up and unified in the more general category of pastoral supervision. Priests and deacons are then considered to share in the bishops' pastoral care by reason of their ordination.

One result of this broad approach has been a tendency among ecumenically-minded clergy to define the sacrament of orders in terms of the ministry of the word in all its many forms. If the intention is to give a description of the life of ordained ministers there is much to recommend this point of view, since both bishops and priests devote the major part of their time and attention to the word and to the organization of the community to whom the word is addressed; and the function of deacons too is best understood in these terms. The strictly sacramental role of bishops and priests is then easily integrated into their ministry of the word and there are obvious pastoral reasons for underlining the continuity between the two.

There are, however, much stronger theological reasons for proposing that it is the sacramental role of ordained ministers that should be made central to an adequate, that is, christological, understanding of their function in the church. This is not, of course, to suggest that the Catholic church's refound emphasis on the word ought to be seen as questionable. It may well, in fact, be that the largely unstructured character of the ministry of the word, not to speak of ecclesiastical administration, needs to find a strong psychological anchor in the minister's eucharistic office. The fundamental reasons, however, for placing the Eucharist at the center of the ordained minister's service to the church are the same as those which make the Eucharist the center of the life of the church.

All the ministries, those of the laity as well as those of the clergy, are exercised in the name of Christ and through the Spirit, and they are for the development of the church as the sacrament in the world of the Blessed Trinity. Clearly, then, all of them turn on the sacramental presence of Christ himself in the Eucharist; and the ministry of the priest or bishop, which is in direct function of this presence, must be understood theologically

194 A General Theory of the Sacramental System

in terms of it. To lay claim, in virtue of the Spirit, to ministry of whatever kind, and to fail to relate this to the Eucharist, betrays lack of sensibility for the way of life of the Christian community and conceals the germ of error about the Trinity.

The historical development of the ordained ministry needs to be interpreted in the light of the principle just enunciated, for it is service to the eucharistic community that provides the unequivocal link that binds the present ministry to the invitation issued by Christ at the last supper that the apostles should preserve his memory in this way. The most remarkable characteristic of the history of the ministry is, in fact, the rapid consensus reached in the post-apostolic church on precisely this interpretation. It is not being argued that a "priest" is one who offers sacrifice and that, therefore, priests are ordained for the Eucharist. There is no place for such false analogies with the priesthood of the Old Testament; and, in any case, as has been seen (cf. 4.5), the sense in which the Eucharist is understood to be a sacrifice requires careful clarification. It is much more simple than that, as a matter of such vital importance to the Christian churches must be. The heart of the matter is the sacramental presence of Christ, the incarnate Word, in the community and the ministry given by him for it to be brought about.

The need for the Eucharist in the community is such that the sacrament of orders must evidently be an abiding sacrament. On analogy with baptism, the abiding sacrament or character constitutes the specific gift given by the Spirit when the sacrament is conferred, a gift which this time is in favor of the community. The distinction made by St. Augustine between abiding sacrament and personal grace in the case of baptism is of even more importance here where it is the christological basis of the community that is to be provided for. The constant appeal of reforming movements within Christianity to a ministry of the Spirit, understood as one that is validated exclusively by personal sanctity or, oddly, by observance of the Law, has uniformly been rejected by the Catholic tradition. This has obviously nothing to do with any hesitations about the need for a pious clergy, but derives from a conviction that the gift of the Spirit to the community is inextricably linked with the personal mission of the divine Word and its sacramental continuation in the Eucharist. The emphasis is on Christ, on his initiative, and on the provision he has made for the permanence of the Eucharist in the community; to ensure this the abiding sacrament of orders is indispensable.

The abiding sacrament, even more clearly than in the case of baptism, can only be given by the risen Christ who, through it, brings the priest into a permanent relationship with himself in view of his own personal entry into the community in the Eucharist. The Catholic understanding of the real presence is such that, without the intervention of the creative power of the incarnate Word, neither the Eucharist itself nor the ministry of the Eucharist is conceivable. This is what is implied by insistence on the abiding character or sacrament of orders.

It is sometimes called in question today for pastoral reasons, the quite valid point being made that in certain circumstances the church will have to devise a form of ministry having little in common with the one that is known at present in the more developed areas of the world. It has to be understood, however, that the sociological structure of the ordained ministry, whether it is a full-time or part-time activity, whether it is exercised by clerical specialists or by those who are principally engaged in other social functions, is a matter for pastoral initiative or personal calling. The need for the abiding sacrament of orders, on the contrary, is one that is held to derive from the christological structure of the church and, therefore from the very nature of divine salvation. Whatever be the life-style that the minister of the Eucharist may have to adopt in the circumstances envisaged (and this is not a matter that can be convincingly discussed by European or North-American theologians), he cannot be a minister of the Eucharist if the risen Christ has not intervened to make him such through the sacrament in which the church has recognized his active presence for this purpose.

Because of the categories they were familiar with, the Scholastics usually spoke of the priestly character as a "power," adding that it was one placed at the service of Christ for the community. The point they were making is evident enough in the light of the representative role that is assigned the ordained minister in the Eucharist where he symbolizes the presence of Christ, the unique mediator, and speaks in his name the words of institution. The Catholic community in the West today is probably more conscious, or becoming so, that, since the priest's role here is a ministerial one, the invocation of the Spirit accompanying the eucharistic words is not an empty formula. Only Christ, in virtue of his mission from the Father, can send the Spirit with authority, and the Eucharist itself is a gift of the Spirit. What seems to be less emphasized in the Eastern tradition is that the character too is a gift of the Spirit, one that relates the ordained priest in a stable way to the misson of the Word in the sacramental church. The character can be effective in the mystery of the Eucharist only if the action of the minister is taken up into the movement of divine creative love that maintains Christ in his role as mediator and that reaches its fulfilment only when those who approach the Eucharist so consecrated are drawn into communion with the Blessed Trinity.

Sufficient has been said in this general approach to indicate that the special intervention of Christ in the sacrament of orders is directed immediately to the giving of the priestly character, the abiding sacrament, and that this, in its turn, is directed towards the Eucharist.

In a more detailed study of orders it would be necessary to show how the pastoral care of bishops, which includes the conferring of orders, is also centered on eucharistic service. It might then be a question as to the sense in which the diaconate is considered to be sacramental.

8.1.3 Confirmation

Though confirmation forms part of Christian initiation, it is more helpful to consider it after marriage and orders since these indicate two typical ways in which it is actually called into play in the life of the church. Despite what must be considered exhaustive research into the history of confirmation, carried out in recent years, a definition of its significance has proved elusive. It is traditionally associated with the gift of the Spirit but this, of course, does nothing to distinguish it from any other gift granted to the church. Since the hypothesis we are following is that the direct efficacy and significance of the sacraments is to be sought in the abiding sacrament, and that the gift of the sanctifying Spirit, grace, can be discussed only in terms of the individual's personal assimilation of that gift, it must be seen whether this can be verified in the case of confirmation. This may not prove anything, but it may indicate a certain coherence and explanatory value in the hypothesis.

The reason, so it appears, for the lack of precision in what is usually said about confirmation is that the traditional understanding, with its references to the Spirit, to maturity and to mission, is interpreted in terms of what Catholics sometimes call sacramental grace, which is not essentially different from sanctifying grace. This, quite naturally, raises difficulties about baptism which is also considered in terms of the justification and sanctification bestowed through it, and so in terms of the Spirit. It is at this point that it is useful to recall once again St. Augustine's distinction between the plenary effects of baptism and its abiding sacrament. When this is applied to confirmation and discussion turned to the significance of its abiding sacrament, there may be some hope of suggesting an objective, though perhaps not absolute, distinction between the two sacraments of initiation. In discussing the character of confirmation it is necessary to proceed by way of analogy with the character of baptism, though it may be enlightening to look also to the abiding sacrament of other sacraments.

The analogy with baptism and orders has long suggested that the character of confirmation should be understood as a sharing in the priesthood of Christ as it is exercised in the church. As the discussion of the Eucharist shows, the faithful's common priesthood is exercised in what the New Testament calls spiritual sacrifice, and the characters of orders and baptism have their respective roles to play in bringing that sacrifice into union with Christ's in the Eucharist.

It is not so easy to see how a third character, that of confirmation, can give some further share in Christ's priesthood, it being understood that any explanation will have to be in terms of sacramental union with Christ. To say, for example, that this character allows a form of sacramental participation that corresponds to adult status in the church is not really to say anything, for Christian maturity is something that must be explained in terms of grace and the personal development of the individual. It seems better not to insist, in the case of confirmation, on a specific relationship established through the character with Christ's priesthood. The title of priest, like any other title applied to Christ, has only an analogical value; it underlines one aspect of Christ's mission in terms of what the New-Testament writers took to be more readily comprehensible to its readers. The broadest category that can be found for Christ's mission is that of "mediator," for it can be taken as including all the other more specific titles attributed to him. Now, it does not appear superfluous to suggest that a special form of sacramental union with Christ might be given which imparts a particular way of sharing in his broad mission of mediation; and this might then be attributed to the character of confirmation.

The kind of sacramental incorporation here envisaged is not one that is required for sharing in the strictly sacramental actions of Christ and the church; baptism and orders suffice for that. It should be thought of rather as the granting and acceptance of status in the church as a general sacrament. Once again, baptism suffices for incorporation into the church as sacrament of the Blessed Trinity, and it carries with it the personal obligation of making that sacrament a living and efficacious one. This does not exclude a new relationship being set up between the confirmed person and Christ as the one sent by the Father as mediator of salvation. It carries with it an obligation to bring Christ's mediation into all the circumstances of the Christian's life in society, an obligation deriving from representative status in the church. This would explain why confirmation is presupposed to, and specified by, the sacraments of marriage and orders, both of which give new forms of official standing in the church.

The history of the rites of initiation shows clearly enough that too much should not be made of the distinction between baptism and confirmation. The symbolism of the latter, however suggestive it proved to the Fathers, both Greek and Latin, remains imprecise and the status given by its character is hardly to be thought of as essentially different from that given in baptism, though it does make explicit, and requires acceptance of, its public, missionary dimension. It might be legitimate to grant that, in this case, the character is a purely moral entity in the sense that the one who bears it is given new responsibilities in Christian living. This was the solution that has to be judged inadequate in the case of baptism and orders where the assimilation they give to the risen Christ is understood as brought about by his power to renew all creation. The realism of Christ's entry into the Eucharist, which was held to require the ontological reality of those two characters, is, precisely, not a factor that has to be considered in the case of confirmation.

Once it is grasped that the term "sacrament" is analogical and therefore does not imply any strict uniformity among the events to which it is applied, an appreciable amount of flexibility becomes permissible and necessary in interpreting it if the circumstances of a particular sacrament require or suggest this. If stress were to be laid on the action of the risen Christ as a necessary element of a sacrament in the strict sense—which was the preliminary hypothesis formulated above—then it might reasonably be argued that confirmation is strictly sacramental only when it is taken in conjunction with baptism or, what amounts to the same thing, that the two form one complex sacrament. If the abiding sacrament of confirmation is understood as a moral entity, a new responsibility, then it simply opens a new dimension of activity to the person who already bears the character of baptism, and an active intervention of Christ is called for only when baptism is given.

The fact that the local bishop should properly admit candidates to confirmation argues in favor of seeing this rite as an official act of the church which gives full play to the sacramental incorporation of baptism. When stress is laid instead on the abiding sacrament and it is understood as a moral entity, then it seems legitimate to go further and say that, in the case of confirmation, the church has, for pastoral reasons, allowed the unique sacrament of initiation to develop into two distinct rituals. Each of these is called a sacrament but the second is such only because it was already included in the original rite of initiation. It is the integral sacrament that is "instituted" by Christ, this being understood in the sense that the full sacrament of initiation is pre-supposed to the community of the church because it depends for its efficacy on the risen Christ.

To be officially associated with the mission of the church is to share in the mediatorial role of Christ who sends the Spirit into the world. It was for this role that Christ himself received the Spirit when he was on earth; and it is for this reason that confirmation may be called, in a special way, the sacrament of the Spirit. Whatever is said in the Catholic tradition about the sacrament conferring the sanctifying Spirit must, however, be inter-preted in strictly personalist terms. It is not, in any case, for this reason that confirmation is referred to the Spirit. Once again, too much should not be made of the passing ceremony as a unique occasion of grace, though nothing prevents its being such. The abiding sacrament possesses that dynamic quality that the person who bears it gives it; in this way it is related to the constantly recurring sacra-ment of the Eucharist in which Christ comes for no other reason than to give the Spirit and to gather up into his own worship those spiritual sacrifices that, for the confirmed, have a new significance.

8.1.4 Anointing of the sick and dying

When, as is normal, anointing of the gravely ill or aged is accompanied by, or closely associated with, the sacra-ments of penance and the Eucharist, it is difficult to offer a convincing account of it in terms of "sanctifying grace" for, as always, the coming of Christ in the Eucharist is the all-encompassing offer of grace. The special signif-icance of anointing must be sought, first of all, in the ministry of the word surrounding it, not only in the ceremony itself but in the whole pastoral care offered to the sick, and then in the symbolism of the sacrament. Both word and symbolic action invite those who suffer to discover within their own present experience the existential significance of the Christian approach to sickness and death; and there is every reason to believe that Christ, to whom the sick person is commended, uses word and symbol and the experience to which they are addressed, as ways of drawing to himself those who suffer. But all of this, by itself, does not account for anointing being numbered among the sacraments in the strict sense.

Once again, sacramentality must be explained by reference to an abiding sacrament, a special form of incorporation into the church-sacrament. Suffering has clearly a special significance in the church of the crucified Christ, as has already appeared in the discussion of Christ's satisfaction for sin (cf. 2.3.3) and of the Eucharist as sacrifice (cf. 4.3; 4.5). It is recognized as evil and the message of the resurrection is that it has been overcome, together with death, by Christ. The fact that it remains is at once a temptation to doubt and an opportunity to enter personally into the mystery of the suffering Christ and to bear witness to his victory.

It seems reasonable, then, to suggest that anointing involves a recognition of the special place that the sick and the dying have in the church as sacrament of Christ the mediator. The merging of reality and sacrament is similar to what happens in penance with which anointing has a close affinity. The further efficacy of the sacrament is not well defined. The rite of anointing prays that "the Lord who frees you from sin save you and raise you up," using the words of *James*, 5:15. Such lack of precision is in the nature of the case where a broad appeal is made to the love and mercy of the risen Christ that he may send the grace of the Spirit. Christ has it in his power to restore even bodily health; but the only certain promise that he has made about it is that he will bring final bodily resurrection.

He has it in his power too, to "raise up" the Christian faith and hope of the sufferer so that, in ways that remain incomprehensible to the bystander, he may experience a deeper healing of his personality. It is just in this way that Christ's "satisfaction" becomes a meaningful reality in the world when those who believe free themselves from whatever it is that has its origin in evil and stands in the way of the individual and of mankind becoming true images of God. None of this is the work of a moment; it asks too much and the lesson is not an easy one to learn. The Christ who comes in the Eucharist comes to make it possible and to resolve the crisis. There is an abiding sacrament but it appears to be one that is given through the prayers of the church and the solemn commendation of the sick person to the special care of Christ. While this fulfils all the demands that Christ himself made for a prayer that will always be answered, it does not require that special intervention of Christ, acting through the materiality of the world that is found in, for example, baptism or the Eucharist.

The abiding sacramentality of grave illness merges, in fact, with the reality of the sick person's situation in a way that has been remarked on in the case of marriage. The sacramentality of marriage was found to be rooted in the closeness of man and wife to the mystery of creation, reaffirmed in Christ. Sickness and death affect the same unfathomable recesses of the human person, and death permits appeal to no one but to the risen Christ. It is perhaps this ultimate and unavoidable outcome of Christian life, where salvation alone can give meaning, that justifies numbering anointing among the sacraments.

8.2 A GENERAL THEORY OF THE SACRAMENTS

The sheer variety of the events that are known as sacraments serves as a warning against any too rapid attempt at formulating a definition applicable to all of them. Indeed, the history of the search for a general definition, beginning with St. Augustine and culminating in the treatises of the twelfth and thirteenth centuries, is the story of how an intuition of faith struggled to find words that would be adequate to express both the depth and the breadth of the mystery of the sacramental Christ and his saving activity in the church.

The intuition had to do with the way in which God comes to meet sinful man, first in the person of Christ, then in the actions of the church. For Augustine this could be summed up as the self-communication of God through images and signs so that sacrament could be said to be (as later theologians summarized his view) "the visible form of invisible grace." So abstract a definition could obviously have significance only for those who shared in the life of a community of believers centered on the celebration of the Eucharist and structured by the preaching of the word and by all the symbolism of liturgical worship. It was within the hermeneutic context of this same community life that the theologians of the monasteries and, later, of the medieval universities could remain perfectly intelligible when they made proposals for refining Augustine's intuition, when they added to its terms or suggested complementary points of view, derived for the most part from other writings of Augustine himself.

There was no sense of innovation, only, so it would seem, general recognition of the obvious, when Hugh of St. Victor (died, 1141) made the point that the sacraments his colleagues were attempting to define could not be adequately grasped in terms of signification, that is was necessary to take explicit note of their "efficacy," *efficacia*. He found less ready acceptance for the unsubtle metaphor he used, picturing the sacraments as "vessels containing grace," though the image was, in fact, destined to enjoy a theological career all its own and to mislead many. A more cautious expression was soon put forward with the phrase, "the sacrament 'confers' the invisible grace or sacred things that it signifies" (*Summa sententiarum*, 12th cent.). This proved acceptable and was still used at the Council of Trent. Debate was, however, principally reserved in the twelfth and thirteenth centuries for the suggestion of the influential Peter of Lombardy that the efficacy admitted by all should be understood as efficient causality; for, as he put it, sacraments are given not only for their symbolic value but also in order to sanctify.

This was a matter that called for further clarification, but already the agreement about efficacy had made it possible to identify which of the community's accepted practices adequately satisfied the definition. It may not have been made clear exactly how each of them satisfied the definition; but at least other contenders were eliminated. The way was then open for the theologians of the thirteenth century to develop a more systematic discussion of the seven sacraments. Not unnaturally, their attention was focussed on baptism, orders and the Eucharist; penance and marriage proved difficult to deal with; and there was a tendency to say of confirmation and anointing that they were "similar" to the others. What was achieved was a broad synthesis linking the sacraments with the mystery of Christ and with the life of Christians.

The situation today is clearly very different for the background of a common liturgy in which all parties to the discussion share is no longer an explicit presupposition to theological thinking. An attempt now has to be made to rediscover the significance of the sacraments as structural elements integral to the Christian life. An abstract definition is useless if it cannot be related in a personal way to the rich and changing variety of ordinary experience. For this reason the post-medieval theological treatise on the sacraments "in general" hardly forms a fit subject for contemporary theological curricula unless it is woven into an examination of individual sacraments.

It was in order to avoid speaking abstractly about abstractions that marriage was introduced first in these pages as the most revealing example there is of the sacramental idea, for in it reality, when it succeeds, is the sacrament.

It still remains that the fullness of sacrament is to be found only in the Eucharist; for this reason a general statement about sacraments should be such that it reflects this primary example. In fact, it is more than an example. Its symbolism, both as communion and as sacrifice, spells out for faith the totality of the Christian mystery: "The fact that there is only one loaf means that, though there are many of us, we form a single body because we all have a share in this one loaf" (1 Cor 10:17). Through the medium of the symbolism the risen Christ joins himself with his commuinty: "Until the Lord comes, therefore, every time you eat this bread and drink this cup, you are proclaiming his death, and so anyone who eats the bread or drinks the cup of the Lord unworthily will be behaving unworthily towards the body and blood of the Lord" (1 Cor 11:16-27). And because Christ is present, what the symbolism spells out and promotes is to be brought about.

There is an obvious difficulty about devising a definition that would apply to the fullness of the Eucharist and in addition to all the other sacraments, each with its own particular significance. This was, perhaps, a weakness inherent in the task that the medieval theologians set themselves for, though they understood that none of the other sacraments is equal in dignity to the Eucharist, and though they grasped that this meant that the others are to be seen in their relation to it, they still persisted in looking for a common denominator justifying a general definition. They would, of course, have been the first to insist that their definition was to be predicated analogically of the individual sacraments; but not everyone today shares the delight in Aristotelian logic that such a disclaimer reveals and that made the disclaimer necessary in the first place. In any case, it still remains to inquire just how each sacrament corresponds to the analogical definition.

It is in conformity with the facts to treat the sacraments as a system, having a structure that culminates in the Eucharist, with each of the others either being directly intelligible in terms of the Eucharist or so shaping human life in Christ as to endow it with meaning that calls out for that union with Christ that only the Eucharist can give. The Eucharist then will shed its light on the others, for they are either intrinsic to the eucharistic mystery or participate in its fullness by making explicit, where the life of the church requires it, what Christ's sacramental union with the church implies. It must not be forgotten that this whole system is given to the church so that it may become the sacrament of the Blessed Trinity, and that the church exists, not for itself alone, but in and for the world. The world, indeed, is more properly seen as being in the church of the Eucharist, for the church is the place where the mystery of Christ, which is everywhere at work through the Spirit, is explicitly announced and celebrated. When the church preaches and receives the word and celebrates it in the Eucharist, it is bringing into focus the true meaning of all human life, a meaning that the church itself does not give, but one that is written in the heart of every person who issues from the hand of the Father, brought into being by his divine love through the Word, and so created in the image of God.

The sacramental system is not, therefore, for a closed circle of initiates. It is a gathering into coherence of all the strands of meaning that are discoverable in human existence. It is not that the coherence has already been established in Christian life for, evidently, it has not, or has, at best, been achieved only in fragmentary fashion, except in the case of those who are recognized as saints. The word of the gospel shows where coherence

is to be found; and in the sacraments moments of unambiguous harmony can occur when the risen Christ
takes the initiative and allows mankind to grasp, however fleetingly, something of what he meant when he said
that he would draw all things to himself.

8.2.1 Professions of faith

One characteristic is common to all the elements of
the sacramental system, though it is not distinctive. All
the sacramental sign-actions and ways of life are manifestations of the faith of the church; and without the
faith of the community, there can be no sacraments.
"Whence this power of water so exalted as to bathe the
body and cleanse the soul, if it is not through the action
of the word; not because it is spoken, but because it is
believed?" (St. Augustine, *On the Gospel of John*, tr. 80,
3; Palmer, 127). The sacraments are, indeed, presupposed
to the community of believers to the degree that they
depend on Christ, the unique Mediator. Nevertheless,
it is by faith that any symbolic activity of the community
or any Christian way of life is brought into relation
with the person of Christ and the salvation he offers. Even
when the individual on whom a sacrament of faith is
conferred is, for one reason or another, incapable of a
personal act of faith, the faith of the community is active,
taking up the individual and offering him to the mercy
of Christ.

In sacramental practice the salient aspect of faith
that is brought to light in prayer is the church's total
dependence on Christ, the mediator who holds from the
Father the mission of sending the Spirit on mankind to
draw it away from sin and into the mystery of the Trinity.
In a living refusal of all forms of Pelagianism, the church
affirms in the sacraments that faith itself is a gift of the
Spirit, awakened by the word of the gospel in the heart of
the individual. Because there is faith, there is worship
in union with Christ, and a pleading for grace to preserve
the union.

Word and symbol shape the community's faith so that it is the whole mystery of salvation, past, future and present, with all that it implies by way of gift and by way of obligation, that is being rehearsed and celebrated; and none of this can be done if the Spirit is not already present in the church which is his creation. The words and symbols of each sacrament, together with the way of life, the human realism, that each one implies, give to each its own special significance in the mystery. Only the Eucharist reaches out, in its symbolic activity and in the faith it evokes, to the universality of the mystery of Christ; for this reason the other sacraments, even as professions of the community's faith and worship and as prayers for the Spirit, look to the Eucharist for their completion.

8.2.2 *Efficacy from the risen Christ*

The Eucharist permits the clearest statement of how these lived professions of faith differ from preaching and the hearing of the word and from all the other ways in which the church prays for the Spirit or gives practical effect to its convictions. In it alone, Christ comes in person—in the realism of his risen being—into the symbolic space created by the community's act of faith and adoration that draws its authenticity from the realism of the spiritual sacrifices of the faithful. In the action of the Eucharist he unites into one the Christian sacrifices and gives himself as the bearer of the Spirit in communion; in the sacrament he remains permanently within the community, a constant point of reference for all its activity. Christ's lordship extends to the giving of the Spirit and to the transformation of the material world; the Eucharist shows that his cosmic power is not held in suspense until the end of time. When the words of institution are spoken in his name and in the power of the Spirit, the abiding sacrament of the Eucharist, the real presence of Christ, is brought into the community of believers.

In the Eucharist, it is the real presence of Christ that constitutes the immediate and certain efficacy of the sacrament. It can be accounted for only in terms of the power of the risen Christ, but its whole purpose lies in the community, which Christ comes to form as his body, which was present in him on Calvary and which is now to fill up what is lacking from his sufferings so that it may come to be with him in glory. Because Christ's mission is universal, the Eucharist has significance for all members of the human race for in it is gathered together the mystery of salvation in its present phase.

If the community of the church is privileged to share in this unambiguous proclamation of the Lord it is not because it forms the assembly of the elect. It is because it has been called to a representative role, one which demands that its members hear the word and respond to it, one which certainly imposes a mission on its members, but also one which mysteriously makes of the assembly a place in which thanksgiving is offered for the Spirit who is sent to all who are ready to listen to the voice of conscience, a place in which supplication is made in Christ for all. The Eucharist is never an empty ritual for the community of the church and the wide community of the human race is always associated with its Savior. For all that, the community's part is necessarily a personal one, as was Mary's at Calvary. The grace that is given is not grace until it has become active participation of the members in the mystery of Christ.

The way in which efficacy is attributed to the Eucharist points the way towards the account that should be given of the efficacy of the other sacraments. In each case it is the abiding sacrament that is always given if the sacrament is given. In each case, though not always in the same way, there is an offer of grace which becomes grace only when it has been transposed into personal response. In baptism and orders, the characters assimilate their bearers to the risen Christ who is personally active in these sign-actions of the church to incorporate those who receive them into his sacramental body. As members whose faith is sacramentalized, they are drawn into that area of salvation where the Eucharist and the other sacraments are celebrated and in which the ordained priest serves the community as Christ's sacramental representative.

In marriage and penance, where the abiding sacrament and its ecclesial significance are rooted in personal decisions of the participants, the immediate intervention of Christ is not always indicated. The bond of marriage is an integral element of the promises exchanged, when they are made in Christ. Sorrow for sin may be given by the Spirit outside the sacrament of penance; when it is sacramentalized, as its dependence on Christ and the economy of salvation require, the intervention of Christ cannot be made the subject of a generalization. In confirmation, too, it seems to be sufficient to see the abiding sacrament as a development of the baptismal character, with the local bishop accepting and confirming the candidate's readiness to serve Christ the Mediator in the church's mission of bearing witness to the gospel. Likewise, anointing of the sick, which recognizes the special significance of suffering and death for the church of the crucified Christ, and confers a corresponding position in the church, is addressed to Christ as a community prayer; the form that his response will take is not fully determined by the sacrament.

The abiding sacrament, in all its varied forms, is that which is given whenever the sacrament itself is given. It may already belong to the personal order, as it clearly does in marriage, or even to the order of sanctifying grace, as it always does in penance and often does in anointing; or it may be an absolute gift of the risen Christ as in the Eucharist, in baptism and orders. In every case it is a gift of the Spirit. The Spirit's action is echoed in personal response even when the characters of baptism and orders are given, for the community is active in both sacraments and, at least in orders, the individual has made a personal decision.

The conferring of sanctifying grace, however, must be understood in fully personal terms. It is always a free gift of God and it is always to be personalized by the one who receives it, to the degree that that person is capable of personal action. The conferral of sacraments on infants or on those who appear to be unconscious has not to be discussed here; but it is clear that the influence of the Spirit is not confined to those levels of consciousness we take to be signs of maturity. In any case, the mystery of grace, in which the absolute initiative is God's, becomes existentially relevant to the individual only when he gives himself to God with all the freedom he commands. It is only then that he recognizes—not theoretically but in thanksgiving—that his own life has resolved the paradox of grace.

8.2.3 *The sending of the Spirit*

It may well be that Catholic theologians in the past, hewing too closely to Trent's condemnations of a mosaic of texts drawn from the Reformers' writings, took the personalism of grace too much for granted and developed unilaterally the initiative of Christ that is foremost in the symbolism of the sacraments. The human side of grace was made sufficiently clear in Trent's decree on justification and was developed in authentic Catholic moral theology which had not degenerated into a casuistry of sin. Writers on the sacraments expended much effort and displayed awesome finesse in their discussions of what was called "sacramental grace," of how it differed from "ordinary" sanctifying grace, and of how the particular grace of each sacrament differed from the special graces of the others. Now, all of this could have been settled in a thoroughly satisfactory manner by saying that God is a personal God and that he addresses himself to persons.

Nevertheless, the question of the definition of "sacramental grace" became one of the "classical" problems of post-medieval theology and was accepted by serious theologians as a serious one. The very way it was placed, whatever subtlety any answer relied on, focussed attention on sanctifying grace as the specific object of the efficacy of the sacraments. As well as this, theologians of the Thomist school became so fascinated with Aquinas's intuition concerning the way in which Christ is active through the very materiality of sacraments that it was only in the comparatively recent past that they began to pay attention to the active participation of the faithful in the Mass and the sacraments. Even then the center of interest was usually Christ's giving of the Spirit. Certainly they did not show any awareness in their treatises on the sacraments "in general" that sacraments differ so much among themselves that the authentic intuition of St. Thomas ought to be reserved to the major sacraments.

Though the efficacy of the sacraments has been directly related to the gift of the abiding sacrament, this does not imply that sacraments cannot be moments of grace when the Spirit is given. The contrary is true, for sacrament is always meant to be the correlate of reality. But grace is given to a responsible person only when he is acting as a responsible person. As well as this, there are strong reasons for looking at the grace associated with the sacraments in terms of the Eucharist-centered system formed by the sacraments themselves; and this serves to underline the personalism of grace. When, as is normal, the celebration of the other sacraments is set within the liturgy of the Eucharist, it is clearly to the Eucharist that we should look as to the culminating moment of grace. It is in the spiritual sacrifice and communion of the Eucharist that Christ comes in person to give the Spirit to those who are entering into a new state of life or have taken up again their Christian obligations.

There has never been any hesitation about the need for personal response and commitment when the building of the body of Christ through the Eucharist is discussed. If we pursue the implications of this, and break away from the artificiality imposed by the ill-considered attempt of Catholic theologians to distinguish seven "kinds" of sanctifying grace, then the realization will emerge that all so-called sacramental grace, whenever and however it is given and received, is a sharing in the one Spirit offered by the one eucharistic Christ. The thought may be pushed even further, and the effort made to envisage the full implications of the coming of the incarnate Word in the Eucharist. Since his presence is wholly personal, it is in the Eucharist that all salvation in the time of the church is to be found, for nowhere else is the risen Christ to be found in the fullness of his saving mission.

The point has been made several times in these pages that the risen Christ sends his Spirit to all mankind by way of the deepest recesses of human personality and human community, for in no other way can his universal mediation be accounted for. The church has then to be seen as the place where Christ's word and sacraments are explicitly recognized and celebrated. It is now being suggested that the church of the Eucharist is more than the coming to consciousness of the mystery of Christ. To this Eucharist as to its source must be attached the giving of the Spirit in all its universality, for in the Eucharist is the total presence of Christ "for you" and "for all." Until Christ comes, his death, with all that it implies, is proclaimed here, so that here is the Christ who is actively saving all men, and to him, as he is here, all the gifts of the Spirit are inescapably drawn.

If this is the mystery of the eucharistic body of Christ as it affects all salvation, then it becomes evident that whatever grace the tradition has been accustomed to associating with the individual sacraments is in fact a sharing in the grace of the Eucharist. This does not detract from the specific and personal character of the other sacraments, in particular that of marriage and penance, with all the realism that they have been seen to imply. The fidelity and love of married life, the struggle to be true to sorrow, these remain rooted in the fabric of daily life; but it is just these personal qualities that call out to the Christ of the Eucharist and bring their realism to its celebration.

8.2.4 The system

It is now possible to discern more clearly the structure of the sacramental system. Its significance is to be discovered in the personal union it establishes between the risen Christ and mankind, and in particular with the assembly of believers who form the church. Its purpose is to bring into being and to promote the church as the living sacrament of the saving design of the Blessed Trinity which restores its creature to authentic humanity and raises it up to a union of life with the three divine Persons. In the Eucharist the whole mystery of the creative and redemptive Trinity is concentrated, for here the incarnate Word continues his mission in the world, as he takes up the worship and the spiritual sacrifice of his community, his body on earth, and unites them with his heavenly worship of the Father, and continues to send his Spirit as an integral function of his commerce with the Father. The specific gift of the Eucharist is the sacramental presence of the risen Christ within the space created by the community's worship, in the form of bread and wine. From this body the church springs; without this body the church, even though it maintained the ministry of the word and fostered Christian fellowship, would not be the integral body of Christ on earth.

Each of the other sacraments, in so far as it bestows an abiding sacrament, contributes to the sacramentality of the church. The baptismal character incorporates into the assembly of the Eucharist; the grace of justification and divine sonship associated with, but not restricted to, baptism is, in fact, already a sharing in the grace of the Eucharist, saving incorporation into the body of Christ and participation in the life of the Trinity.

The character of orders gives that assimilation to the risen Christ which, when the community is at worship and calling upon the Spirit, assures the eucharistic presence. The character of confirmation associates the mature Christian with the church's mission, exercised in the name of Christ the Mediator. The abiding sacrament of the fullness of orders, given in episcopal ordination, associates its bearer with the college of bishops, charged with the pastoral organization of the eucharistic community and, in particular, of the ministry of the word. It is in the college of bishops that the ministry of the word and the ministry of the sacraments coalesce. Because priests are ministers of the Eucharist, they are also, in association with the college of bishops, ministers of the word and of penance. Deacons can be given a share in the pastoral care of the bishop, in particular when they are permitted to preach the word in the liturgical assembly of the Eucharist.

Marriage and anointing, while both are taken up into the all-embracing significance of the Eucharist, bring into the explicit sacramentality of the church the created values and experiences healed by Christ. Clearly, confirmation and orders also do this, since it is the whole personality of the believer that is called to serve in the specifically Christian way of life these sacraments initiate. Marriage and anointing, however, reach beyond service to the redemptive role of Christ, and take hold of the mystery of creation itself, in its gift of life and personhood and in its final enigma.

Penance may, at first sight, appear to lie outside the system or, at best, to provide that "second raft" of salvation the Fathers spoke of, its purpose being to restore full communion with Christ and the church once it has been broken. This judgment may be hasty for the first recorded words of Jesus in the Gospel of Mark are: "The kingdom of God is close at hand. Repent, and believe the Good News" (1:15). This suggests a different, and perhaps more adequate, way of construing the sacramental system. If, instead of describing a system spreading out from the Eucharist, we turn our attention to the whole of humanity addressed by Christ, and make this the starting-point, then it is the sacrament of penance that first offers meaning to mankind. Jesus' first word is "repent"; and where there is true sorrow, no matter in what terms it may be consciously formulated, there is found already that gift of the Spirit of Christ that constitutes the abiding sacrament of penance. Already there is, in an individual's sorrow for fault, that inner dynamism towards the church of the sacramental Christ that, because the Word was made flesh, belongs to true sorrow and to all conversion of heart. The way of life of the repentant sinner has been referred to the Eucharist, and this is to be maintained; but its first existential reference is to the sacrament of forgiveness.

Developing this line of thought, and turning to the other human realities that become sacramental in the church, both marriage and the sickness that leads to death look towards the fullness of significance and authenticity that can be given them in the sacraments. At the center of all striving after human meaning is the person of Christ, not simply addressing a word of life to those who will hear, but actively drawing all human beings to himself in the power of the Spirit. Sacramental initiation is the avowal of faith that he is indeed the center; this is already to have grasped what he meant when he said: "Do this in memory of me."

The sacramental system offers a structure of meaning for life, drawing on the wisdom and support of the community, giving body to the word of the gospel, reaching into the depths of the human person, in all his individuality as the image of God and the temple of the Spirit, and in all his efforts to build a common life where communication is based on justice, peace and love. The Eucharist goes further and offers ultimate meaning to life, for it promises bodily resurrection and the renewal of the universe. At the end of the second century, St. Irenaeus was already arguing that the pessimism of the gnostics, who rejected the material world as intrinsically evil, was contradicted by the Eucharist, the pledge of personal immortality. A phrase that he used set up a criterion for Catholic theology, one by which the present theory should also be judged for it was formulated in view of it (*Adversus Haereses*, IV, xviii; Bettenson, *Early*, 96): "Our teaching is in accord with the Eucharist, and the Eucharist in turn confirms the teaching."

INDEX

Abiding sacrament:
—analogous term: 174, 189
—of baptism: **5.3**, 171, 172, 173, 186, 191, 216
—of Eucharist: **4.4**, **6.4**, 93 f, 97 ff, 107 ff, 113, 122, 149 ff, 171, 173 f, 195, 215
—of penance/reconciliation: **7**, 186, 215, 217
—of other sacraments: **8**
Absolution: **7**
Alliance: 59 f, 88, 188; *see* Marriage
Ambrose, St.: 71
Anointing: **8.1.4**, 183, 211, 216
Anselm of Canterbury, St.: 41, 143
Anthropology of sacraments: 9 f, 14; *see* Human sciences; Psychotherapy; Symbols
Anti-sacramentalism: 177 f
Archetype: **3.1**, 95, 97, 140
Aristotle: 28, 125 f, 155, 156, 159, 206
Arles, Council of (314): 130 f
Athanasius, St.: 66
Augustine, St.: 16, 18, 67 f, 94 ff, 104, 108 f, 126, 130 ff, 171, 174, 194, 197 f, 204, 208

Baptism: **5**, 58, 71 f, 172, 183, 186 f, 204, 210 f
—character of: *see* Abiding sacrament
—and confirmation: 197 ff
—effect of: 119, 128 ff
—of infants: 116, 120, 128, 171, 212

—and marriage: 190 ff
—necessity of: 183; *see* Salvation of all
—and penance: 167
—symbolism of: 118 f, 121
Barth, Karl: 116 f
Berengar of Tours: 99 ff
Body of Christ (church): 33, 39 f, 42 f, 95 f,109 f, 123, 124, 206, 210, 214, 215
—one person: 37 f, 47
see Church; Community

Casel, Dom Odo: 121
Catholic tradition:
—and creation: 27 ff
—and sacramentalism: 142, 180 f
—and Spirit, gift of: 195
see Method, theological
Causality of sacraments: *see* Efficacy
Celibacy: 29 f
Chalcedon, Council of: 147
Character, sacramental: *see* Abiding sacrament
Church: passim; **3.3**
—and abiding sacrament: 173 f
—St. Augustine and St. Cyprian on: 133
—and Eucharist: 81 f, 214
—incorporation into: 129, 135 ff, 173 f, 186
—and marriage: 190
—and orders: 195
—and sacraments: 133 f
—as sacramento-real: 134 f

219